365 Slim & Healthy Recipes

© Naumann & Göbel Verlagsgesellschaft mbH
a subsidiary of VEMAG Verlags- und Medien Aktiengesellschaft
Emil-Hoffmann-Str, 1, 50996 Cologne (Germany)
www.vemag-medien.de
Photography: TLC Fotostudio
Translation from German: APE International, Richmond (USA)
Overall production: Naumann & Göbel Verlagsgesellschaft mbH
All rights reserved
Printed in China
ISBN 978-3-625-12664-5

365 Slim & Healthy Recipes

Information and Instructions

- All recipes and ingredients given serve 4, unless otherwise stated.

- Actual preparation times may vary slightly from those stated here. This is due in particular to different methods of preparation, varying working speeds, and the type of oven being used. Additional times, such as longer cooking, cooling and baking times, are not indicated separately.

- The oven should always be preheated to the stated temperature for approximately 10 minutes before beginning to cook the food. In the case of convection ovens, please refer to the manufacturer's information on temperature and timing.

- When a recipe requires the peel of a citrus fruit, please use only organic fruit.

- Always use medium-sized eggs and vegetables (such as onions), unless otherwise stated.

- When pepper is required, use freshly ground black pepper whenever possible.

- Full-fat milk products should be used unless otherwise stated. This means: milk: 3.5%, curd cheese: 40%, yoghurt: 3.5% etc.

- Herbs must always be washed and shaken dry before use.

- Onions and garlic cloves should always be peeled before use, unless otherwise stated in the recipe.

- How to peel tomatoes: score a cross in the skin and remove the stalk base. Then scald the tomatoes with boiling water, pour off the water as soon as the skin begins to peel away, and skin the tomatoes.

- Fruit and vegetables must always be washed and cleaned before being used.

- Berries should be washed before being trimmed and cleaned to prevent water from penetrating and diluting the fruit.

- Meat, fish and seafood should be washed and patted dry before being prepared. When preparing pasta and rice, please always pay attention to the directions on the packet. As a general rule: bring hot water to a rolling boil in a sufficiently large saucepan, add 1 pinch of salt and cook the pasta until al dente. Then drain, rinse briefly in cold water and drain well.

BREAKFAST

SNACKS & SOUPS

SALADS

VEGETARIAN

MEAT

FISH

PASTA, RICE AND POTATOES

DESSERTS

Breakfast

Fruit Cocktail

Dice **2 peeled and cored apples**. Mix together with **4 peeled and diced kiwis, 200 g/7 oz strawberries** cut in half and **2 skinned peaches** with the stones removed and diced. Mix **2 tbsp honey** with the **juice of 1¹/₂ lemons** and **¹/₄ tsp ground vanilla** and pour over the fruit. Allow to stand for 10 minutes. Mix together **2 tbsp pine nuts** and **2 tbsp sesame seeds** and sprinkle over the fruit cocktail.

Preparation time:
approx. 30 Min.,
per serving: approx. 3 g P,
4 g F, 26 g C, 166 kcal

Fruit Muesli with Pears

Roast **4 tbsp sunflower seeds** in a pan without fat. Core and dice **4 pears**. Distribute **12 tbsp oat flakes** between 4 bowls, top with diced pears and drizzle with **4 tbsp honey**. Pour over **600–700 ml/1-1¹⁄₄ pints milk** and serve sprinkled with the sunflower seeds.

Preparation time: approx. 10 Min., per serving: approx. 8 g P, 8 g F, 38 g C, 260 kcal

Scrambled Egg with Salmon

Whisk together **8 eggs, salt, cayenne pepper** and **2 tbsp freshly chopped dill**. Gently fry **3 spring onions** cut into rings in **3 tbsp hot oil**. Add the seasoned eggs and **200 g/7 oz smoked salmon** cut in strips, and cook until the eggs begin to

set. Serve the scrambled egg garnished with **coriander leaves** and accompanied by **fresh wholemeal bread** with **butter**.

Preparation time:
approx. 15 Min.,
per serving: approx. 26 g P, 19 g F,
7 g C, 317 kcal

Crêpes with Salmon

For about 6 crêpes

Prepare a batter with **125 g/4^1/2 oz flour, salt, 1 egg, 100 ml/3^1/2 fl oz milk** and **125 ml/4 fl oz still mineral water**. Bake about 6 crêpes using a total of **25 g/1^1/2 tbsp butter** and keep warm. Gently fry **4 thin slender cleaned leeks** cut into rings in **2 tbsp hot butter**. Season with **salt** and **pepper**, stir in **4 tbsp cream cheese** and **2 tbsp green peppercorns** in brine. Add **8 slices of smoked salmon** cut into strips, and heat. Fill the crêpes with the mixture and serve hot.

Preparation time: approx. 30 Min., per crêpe: approx. 13 g P, 8 g F, 19 g C, 205 kcal

Buttermilk Muesli with Fruit

Cut up **300 g/11 oz mixed fruit** (e.g. strawberries, raspberries, blueberries). Roast **100 g/3½ oz oat flakes** with **1 tbsp sunflower seeds** in a pan without fat. Add **3 tbsp linseed** and remove from heat.

Blend together **600 ml/1 pint buttermilk** and **4 tbsp honey** until smooth and mix with the fruit. Place the oat flake mixture in bowls and pour over the fruit buttermilk.

Preparation time: approx. 15 Min., per serving:
approx. 5 g P, 5 g F, 25 g C, 174 kcal

Bilberry Breakfast Shake

Purée **400 g/14 oz fresh sorted and washed bilberries** with **750 g/ 1 lb 10 oz kefir** in a liquidiser. Add **4 tbsp wheat germ** and **4 tbsp oat flakes**, and sweeten with a little **honey** according to taste. Pour the shake into 4 glasses and serve immediately before the flakes swell.

Preparation time: approx. 15 Min., per serving: approx. 9 g P, 4 g F, 18 g C, 166 kcal

Bread Rolls with Blueberry Curd Cheese

For 12 rolls
200 g/7 oz wheat flour · 130 g/4½ oz sunflower seeds ·
20 g/¾ oz dried yeast · 2½ tbsp sugar · ½ tsp salt · 4 tbsp
sunflower oil · 1 egg yolk · 150 g/5 oz cream curd cheese ·
3 tbsp milk · 6 tbsp blueberry jam · flour for the worktop

Work the flour, 100 g/3½ oz sunflower seeds, yeast, 1 tsp
sugar, salt, oil, and 150 ml/5 fl oz lukewarm water to a smooth
dough. Cover and leave to rise in a warm place for about
10 minutes.
Knead the dough well on a floured worktop, roll out until 2 cm/
¾ in thick, and cut out rounds of 8 cm/3 in.
Place the bread rolls on a baking tray lined with baking paper,
brush with whisked egg yolk and sprinkle with the remaining
sunflower seeds.
Leave the baking tray in a warm place until the bread rolls have
risen. Then bake in the oven at 200°C/390°F/Gas 6 (fan oven
180 °C/355°F Gas 4) for about 15 minutes. Turn halfway
through.
Stir together the curd cheese and remaining sugar. Slice open the
cooled rolls, spread with the curd cheese and blueberry jam, and
serve.

Preparation time: approx. 30 Min., per serving: approx. 6 g P, 7 g F, 15 g C, 160 kcal

TIP
Of course, these delicious rolls also taste good
with any other kind of marmalade or spread.

Pomegranate Jelly

For about 2 250 g/9 oz jars
Cut **1 kg/2 lb 4 oz pomegranate** into small pieces and together with
2 peeled oranges cut into pieces, **1 chopped-up lemon**, **125 ml/4 fl oz
red wine**, **2 vanilla pods** and **2 cinnamon sticks** cook in a pot until soft.
Then pass the mixture through a sieve and top up to 500 ml/18 fl oz with
fruit juice or **water**. Mix the liquid together with **500 g/1 lb 2 oz preserving sugar** and cook at a rolling boil for 4 minutes. Pour the jelly into rinsed
jars and seal tightly.

Preparation time: approx. 25 Min., per serving à 20 g: approx. 2 g P, 1 g F, 9 g C, 58 kcal

Apple Jelly with Rose Petals

For about 3 250 g/9 oz jars
Pour **150 ml/5 fl oz corn schnapps** over **1 handful untreated rose petals** in a bowl and leave to soak overnight. Cook until soft **1 kg/2lb 4 oz peeled, cored and diced apples** together with **2 cinnamon sticks, several cloves,** the **grated peel of 1 untreated lemon, 4 tsp vanilla sugar** and **125 ml/ 4 fl oz each of both white wine** and water. Pass through a sieve and measure out 500 ml/18 fl oz liquid. Top up with **apple juice** if necessary. Bring to the boil with **500 g/1 lb 2 oz preserving sugar**, cook at a rolling boil for 4 minutes and pour into prepared jars. Immediately seal tight.

Preparation time: approx. 35 Min., per serving à 20 g: approx. 1 g P, 1 g F, 4 g C, 38 kcal

Fruit Bread

For about 16 slices

Mix together **175 g/6 oz oat flakes, 75 g/2¹/₂ oz brown sugar, 1 tsp cinnamon, 150 g/5 oz raisins, 100 g/3¹/₂ oz chopped dried figs** and **2 tbsp malt extract**. Stir in **300 ml/11 fl oz unsweetened apple juice**. Add through a sieve **175 g/6 oz wholemeal flour** with **3 tsp baking powder** and work to a smooth dough. Place into a greased loaf tin and bake in the oven for about 1¹/₂ hours at 180°C/355°F/Gas 4 (fan oven 160°C/ 320°F/Gas 3). Turn out onto a rack, allow to cool, then cut into slices. Serve with **fruit spread**.

Preparation time: approx. 30 Min., per slice: approx. 3 g P, 1 g F, 30 g C, 148 kcal

Crêpes with Mango Curd Cheese

Prepare a batter from **125 g/4½ oz flour, 2 tbsp sugar, 1 pinch of salt, 3 eggs, 125 ml/4 fl oz each of both milk** and **water**, as well as **2 tbsp butter**, and allow to stand for 30 minutes.

Mix **250 g/9 oz low-fat curd cheese** with **125 ml/4 fl oz whipped cream, 1 tbsp lemon juice, 2 tsp vanilla sugar** and **300 g/11 oz chopped mango**, cut free of the skin and stone.

Using the batter, make 8 crêpes in **3 tbsp butter**, roll them up and serve with the mango curd cheese.

Preparation time: approx. 30 Min., per serving: approx. 9 g P, 9 g F, 20 g C, 208 kcal

27

Cream Cheese and Olive Spread

Stir together **125 g/4½ oz cream cheese** and **75 g/2½ oz yoghurt** until smooth. Stir in **100 g/3½ oz pitted and chopped black olives**, **1 peeled and finely chopped garlic clove** and **1 bunch of chopped basil**, and season with **pepper**. Pan-roast without oil **1 tsp sesame** and grind to a paste in a mortar with a little **salt**. Fold into the spread. Serve with **wholegrain baguette**.

Preparation time: approx. 15 Min., per serving: approx. 5 g P, 20 g F, 7 g C, 234 kcal

Goat's Cheese Spread with Olives

Using a fork, crush up **250 g/9 oz goat's cheese** in a bowl. Fold in **4 tbsp freshly chopped dill, 1 tbsp freshly chopped chervil, 1 tbsp chopped chives** as well as **8 peeled and crushed cloves of garlic** and **10 chopped pitted olives**. Mix with the **juice of ½ lemon** and **5 tbsp olive oil**. Finally, stir in **2 tbsp milk**. Serve the goat's cheese spread with **toasted flatbread**.

Preparation time: approx. 10 Min., per serving: approx. 12 g P, 27 g F, 10 g C, 335 kcal

Raspberry and Banana Smoothie

Rinse, drain and sort **750 g/1 lb 10 oz raspberries**. Peel **2 bananas** and cut into slices. Purée all the fruit except for 4 raspberries and 4 slices of banana in a liquidiser and mix together with **500 g/1 lb 2 oz natural yoghurt** and **4 tbsp honey**.
Pour the shake into glasses and serve garnished with fruit skewers of raspberries, banana slices and **mint leaves**.

Preparation time: approx. 15 Min., per serving: approx. 7 g P, 5 g F, 40 g C, 257 kcal

Honey Curd Cheese with Almonds

Mix together **400 g/14 oz low-fat curd cheese** with **125 ml/4 fl oz milk**,
2 tbsp honey and the **grated peel of ¹/₂ an untreated lime**.
Fold in **2 tbsp ground almonds** and **1 pinch ground vanilla**. Whisk
4 tbsp cream until stiff and fold into the curd cheese.

Preparation time: approx. 15 Min., per serving: approx. 15 g P, 5 g F, 10 g C, 156 kcal

Orange Buttermilk with Sea Buckthorn

8 tbsp sea buckthorn juice • 600 ml/1 pint buttermilk •
200 ml/7 fl oz freshly pressed orange juice • 8 tbsp wheat
flakes • cornflakes to garnish • 1 orange

Blend together the sea buckthorn juice and the buttermilk in a
liquidiser until foamy. Add the orange juice and wheat flakes and
stir together well. Pour the drink into four glasses and sprinkle
with a few cornflakes. Cut the orange into 4 slices and place one
the rim of each glass.

Preparation time: approx. 15 Min., per serving: approx. 8 g P, 2 g F, 31 g C, 191 kcal

TIP

The small orange-red sea buckthorn berries that grow
on thorny bushes are extremely rich in vitamins.
100 g/3½ oz contain around four times more
vitamin C than an orange or a lemon.

Coffee and Cherry Muffins

For 12 muffins

Mix together **150 g/5 oz flour, 2 tsp baking powder, 1 sachet unsweetened instant coffee, 100 g/3½ oz sugar, 2 tsp vanilla sugar, 1 pinch of salt** and **½ tsp cinnamon**. Beat together **2 eggs, 150 ml/ ¼ pint milk** and **2 tbsp vegetable oil**. Mix together the dry and wet ingredients of the cake dough. Fill **12 paper cake cups** in a muffin tray using ⅔ of the mixture. Spread **200 g/7 oz sour cherries** over the cakes, then top with the remaining mixture. Bake the muffins for around 20 minutes in an oven at 200°C/390°F/Gas 6 (fan oven 180°C/355°F/Gas 4). Allow to stand in the tray for 5 minutes then turn out. Dust with **cocoa powder** and **icing sugar**.

Preparation time: approx. 20 Min., per muffin: approx. 3 g P, 2 g F, 20 g C, 121 kcal

Crêpes with Pistachios

Work together **125 g/4½ oz flour, 2 egg yolks, 250 ml/9 fl oz low-fat milk, 1 tbsp sugar, 1 tsp vanilla sugar** and **75 g/2½ oz chopped pistachios** to make a smooth batter and allow to stand for 20 minutes. Then whisk **2 egg whites** with **1 pinch of salt** until stiff and fold into the batter. Fry 8 thin crêpes, one after another, in a pan using **2–3 tbsp butter**. Brush the finished crêpes with **maple syrup** and serve garnished with chopped pistachios.

Preparation time: approx. 25 Min., per serving: approx. 6 g P, 9 g F, 15 g C, 175 kcal

Curd Cheese Pancakes with Fruit

Mix together to a smooth batter **100 g/3¹/2 oz spelt flour, 3 tbsp semolina, 100 g/3¹/2 oz low-fat curd cheese, 150 ml/¹/4 pint low-fat milk, 2 tbsp Demerara sugar, ½ tsp grated peel of an untreated lemon** and **2 egg yolks**, and allow to stand for 30 minutes. Whisk together **2 egg whites** and **1 pinch of salt** until stiff and fold into the batter.
Fry 8–10 thin golden-brown pancakes, one after another, using **4 tbsp butter.**
Mix together **500 g/1 lb 2 oz mixed berries** (e.g. strawberries, blackberries, raspberries, blackcurrants) with **2 tbsp apple syrup** and serve with the warm pancakes.

Preparation time: approx. 40 Min., per serving: approx. 4 g P, 4 g F, 14 g C, 111 kcal

Buttermilk and Spelt Waffles

For 8 waffles

Whisk together **125 g/4 oz butter** and **4 eggs** until foamy. Mix **250 g/9 oz spelt flour** with **2 tsp baking powder** and alternating with **350 ml/12 fl oz buttermilk** stir into the egg mass.

Fold **50 g/1¾ oz sugar** and **1 pinch of salt** into the batter.

Heat and grease the waffle iron. Use the mixture to bake golden-yellow waffles. Serve with either sugar and **cinnamon** or **curd cheese** with fruit.

Preparation time: approx. 15 Min., per serving: approx. 8 g P, 16 g F, 30 g C, 308 kcal

Blood Orange Marmalade

For approx. 4 250g/9 oz jars
Bring 300 g/11 oz filleted blood orange segments, the grated peel of
1 untreated orange,
200 ml/7 fl oz
freshly pressed
blood orange juice
and 500g/
1 lb 2 oz
preserv-
ing sugar
to the boil in a
pan and cook at a
rolling boil for about
4 minutes. Pour the hot
marmalade into the
rinsed jars and seal
immediately.

Preparation time:
approx. 25 Min.,
per serving à 20 g:
approx. 1 g P,
1 g F, 1 g C, 11 kcal

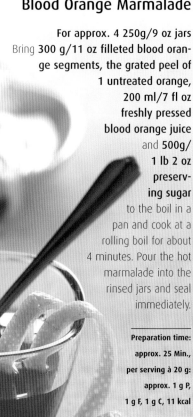

Milk Rolls with Oat Flakes

For 12 rolls

Mix together **400 g/14 oz wheat flour, 100 g/3½ oz oat flakes** (put 2 tbsp of them to one side for later), **1 packet of dried yeast, 1 tbsp honey** and **1 pinch of salt**. Pour in **400 ml/14 fl oz lukewarm milk** less 4 tbsp for later use, knead everything together well and leave covered in a warm place until the dough rises to about twice its size.

Knead the dough well, shape into 12 round rolls and place on a baking tray lined with baking paper. Leave to rise for 10 minutes. Cut a cross into the rolls, brush with the remaining milk and sprinkle with the remaining oat flakes. Bake in the oven at 200°C/390°F/Gas 6 (fan oven 180°C/355°F/Gas 4) for about 20 minutes.

Preparation time: approx. 20 Min., per serving: approx. 5 g P, 2 g F, 31 g C, 170 kcal

Strawberry and Kefir Cornflakes

Clean and trim **600 g/1 lb 5 oz strawberries** and cut into quarters. Mix with **4 tbsp sugar**. Pour **600 ml/1 pint kefir** over the mixture.
Top the strawberry and kefir mixture with **60 g/2 oz cornflakes** and serve immediately while the cornflakes are still crispy.

Preparation time: approx. 15 Min., per serving: approx. 7 g P, 1 g F, 31 g C, 178 kcal

Summer Breakfast

Under constant stirring, roast **80 g/3 oz rolled oat flakes** together
with **4 tbsp sugar** in **4 tbsp butter** until light brown. Put on a plate and
leave to cool.
Wash, trim and quarter **400 g/14 oz strawberries**.
Mix **400 g/14 oz cottage cheese** with the oat flakes, top with the
strawberries and serve.

Preparation time: approx. 10 Min., per serving: approx. 15 g P, 10 g F, 25 g C, 265 kcal

Filled Wholemeal Crêpes

100 g/3^1/$_2$ oz whole wheat flour · 250 ml/9 fl oz low-fat milk ·
3 eggs · 3 tbsp honey · 1 pinch salt · 1 tbsp sunflower oil ·
4 tbsp butter · 2 tbsp sugar · 200 g/7 oz rhubarb ·
100 ml/3^1/$_2$ fl oz cream · 100 g/3^1/$_2$ oz raspberries

Place the flour, eggs, honey and salt in a bowl and stir to a smooth
batter. Last of all, mix in the oil. Heat 2 tbsp butter in a pan and use
the batter to make 6–8 thin crêpes, one after another. Leave to drain
on kitchen towel.

Melt the remaining butter in a pan and while stirring allow the sugar
to caramelise in it. Clean and skin the rhubarb, cut into pieces and add
to the pan. Pour in 100 ml/3^1/$_2$ fl oz water and braise the rhubarb for
15 minutes until soft. Deglaze with the cream. Add the prepared raspberries to the pan and heat through.

Divide the fruit between the crêpes, fold over and serve while still
warm.

Preparation time: approx. 30 Min., per serving: approx. 6 g P, 14 g F, 18 g C, 228 kcal

TIP
You can always replace the rhubarb and
raspberries with other fruit, for example pears
with cinnamon or cherries with mint. Soured milk
can also be used instead of cream.

Fruit and Muesli Trifle

Heat up **100 g/3½ oz each of skinned and stoned apricots, mango and peaches, 40 g/1½ oz dried apple rings** and **25 g/1 oz dried cherries** in a pan together with **450 ml/16 fl oz unsweetened apple juice**. Add **6 cardamom pods, 6 cloves** and **1 cinnamon stick**. Bring the mixture to the boil and simmer for 15 minutes until the fruit is soft. Leave in the pan to cool down.

Remove the spices, purée the fruit and leave to stand in a cool place for about an hour. Pour the purée into dessert glasses, creating alternate layers with **300g/11 oz low-fat yoghurt** and **100 g/3½ oz sugar-free crunchy muesli**. Sprinkle with a little muesli and serve garnished with **wedges of dried fruit**.

Preparation time: approx. 30 Min., per serving: approx. 7 g P, 2 g F, 48 g C, 260 kcal

Orange and Grapefruit Smoothie

Mix together the juice of **1 fresh orange** and **½ grapefruit** with **300 g/ 11 oz yoghurt.**
Whisk until foamy **2 egg yolks** together with **2 tbsp icing sugar** and mix into the orange and grapefruit yoghurt. Stir in **150 ml/¼ pint still mineral water** and divide between 4 large glasses.

Preparation time: approx. 15 Min., per serving: approx. 4 g P, 6 g F, 14 g C, 141 kcal

ACE Drink

For 4 glasses

Briefly dip **2 peaches** in boiling water, remove the skins, remove the stones and dice the flesh of the fruit.

Squeeze the juice from **5 oranges**, cut 1 orange into 4 slices.

Purée the diced peaches with the orange juice, **200 ml/7 fl oz pear juice** and **2 tbsp almond paste**. Divide the drink between four glasses and serve garnished with a slice of orange.

Preparation time: approx. 15 Min., per serving: approx. 3 g P, 3 g F, 38 g C, 208 kcal

Almond and Coconut Spread

Mix together **200 g/7 oz skinned and chopped almonds** with **4 tbsp coconut flakes**, **1 tsp cinnamon** and **10 tbsp maple syrup**.
Fill a jar with the spread. It will keep for about 1 to 2 weeks in the fridge.

Preparation time: approx. 5 Min., per serving: approx. 10 g P, 33 g F, 13 g C, 390 kcal

Greengage Fruit Spread

For 3–4 jars

Stone and purée **500 g/1 lb 2 oz greengages**. Mix with **500 g/1 lb 2 oz preserving sugar** and leave to infuse for 15 minutes. Cut **5 mint leaves** into thin strips and stir into the fruit purée. Bring to the boil in a pan and cook at a rolling boil for 3 minutes. Pour immediately into rinsed screw-top jars. Pour **1 tbsp 54-proof rum** over the surface. Leave standing upside down to cool.

Preparation time: approx. 30 Min., per jar: approx. 13 g P, 1 g F, 18 g C, 91 kcal

Uncooked Berry Spread

For about 3 250 g/9 oz jars

Mix **150 g/5 oz each of strawberries** and **blackberries** (use only flawless fruit) together in a bowl with **250 g/9 oz honey** and place the mixture in the fridge to infuse overnight. Add the **grated peel of 1 untreated lemon**, the **lemon juice** and **40 ml/2½ tbsp raspberry schnapps** to the berries and blend with a hand mixer for about 10 minutes until the honey has dissolved. Fold in **20 g/¾ oz chopped pistachios** and pour the spread into well-rinsed jars. Seal immediately. Store in a cool place.

Preparation time: approx. 20 Min., per serving à 20 g: approx. 1 g P, 1 g F, 5 g C, 30 kcal

Cold Buttermilk Soup with Peaches

500 ml/18 fl oz buttermilk · 300 g/11 oz yoghurt · 4 tbsp
quick oat flakes · 4 tbsp honey · 250 g/9 oz raspberries ·
2 peaches · 4 sprigs of mint

Using a hand mixer, mix the buttermilk, the yoghurt, the oat
flakes and the honey in a bowl until smooth. Sort the raspberries, wash and dab dry.
Cut the peaches in half, remove the stones and dice the peach
halves into small cubes.
Divide the buttermilk mixture between 4 bowls. Top with the
raspberries and peach cubes. Rinse the mint, shake dry and pluck
the leaves from the stems. Serve the cold soup garnished with
the mint leaves.

Preparation time: approx. 10 Min., per serving: approx. 9 g P, 4 g F, 37 g C, 239 kcal

TIP
Buttermilk is an important foodstuff due to the valuable
substances it contains. A cold buttermilk soup is delicious
not only for breakfast but also for lunch on a hot day.

Oat Porridge with Nuts and Maple Syrup

Bring to the boil in a pan **625 ml/1 pint 2 fl oz apple juice, 125 ml/4 fl oz water**, **1/2 tsp ground cinnamon** and **1 pinch of salt**. Add **140 g/5 oz oat flakes, 70 g/ 2 1/2 oz dried cranberries** and **4 tbsp maple syrup** and stir together well. Bring the mixture to the boil and simmer for about 10 minutes while stirring. Fold in **70 g/2 1/2 oz chopped peanuts** and serve accompanied by **whipped cream** sprinkled with **brown sugar**.

Preparation time:
approx. 15 Min.,
per serving:
approx. 9 g P, 13 g F,
49 g C, 357 kcal

Power Drink

For 4 glasses

Rinse and shake dry **1 bunch dill,** put a few sprigs to one side. Then remove the remaining dill from the stalks and chop finely.

Peel **1 cucumber** and cut into rough chunks. Put several thicker slices to one side for use as a garnish.

Blend the cucumber chunks to a purée with the dill, **400 ml/14 fl oz tomato juice, 200 ml/7 fl oz carrot juice** and **1 tbsp olive oil**. Season the drink with **Tabasco sauce** and divide between 4 glasses. Garnish with dill and slices of cucumber.

Preparation time: approx. 10 Min., per serving: approx. 1 g P, 5 g F, 4 g C, 73 kcal

Vitality Bread

For 1 loaf

Soak **30 g/1 oz millet** in water overnight. Drain off excess water.

Prepare a yeast dough using **150 g/5 oz wheat flour, 300 g/11 oz whole wheat flour, 1 packet dried yeast, 1 tbsp honey, 1½ tsp salt** and **30 g/1 oz butter**. Add **30 g/1 oz sunflower seeds, 20 g/¾ oz each of linseed** and **sesame seeds** as well as the millet, **150 g/5 oz yoghurt** and **180 ml/6 fl oz water**, and kneead the dough thoroughly. Place the dough in a warm place to rise.

Knead the dough once again, place in a greased and floured loaf tin and allow to rise for 15 minutes. Place a container filled with water on the floor of the oven. Bake the bread on the bottom rack of the oven for about 45 minutes at 220°C/430°F/Gas 7 (fan oven 200°C/390°F/Gas 6).

Preparation time: approx. 40 Min., per serving: approx. 4 g P, 4 g F, 22 g C, 152 kcal

Mushroom Omelette

Clean **400 g/14 oz mushrooms**, wipe with a damp cloth, cut into quarters and fry until golden brown in **1 tbsp heated rapeseed oil**. Add **1 chopped onion** and **1 chopped garlic clove** and fry together. Remove ³/₄ of the mixture from the pan.

Whisk together **8 eggs** and **100 ml/3¹/₂ fl oz milk**, season with **salt** and **pepper**. Pour ¹/₄ of the egg mixture over the mushrooms in the pan and cook over a medium heat for about 8 minutes until set. Cover with a lid for the last 3 minutes. Keep the finished omelette warm while cooking 3 further omelettes. Serve with **4 tbsp crème fraîche** and **¹/₂ bunch chives** cut into rings.

Preparation time: approx. 15 Min., per serving: approx. 19 g P, 20 g F, 3 g C, 272 kcal

Cherry and Peach Spread

For 5–6 250 g/9 oz jars
500 g/1 lb 2 oz sour cherries • 500 g/1 lb 2 oz vineyard
peaches • 100 g/3½ oz Demerara sugar • 1 packet of gelling
agent for 1 kg/2 lb 4 oz fruit

Wash the cherries and remove the stones. Skin the peaches,
remove the stones and dice the fruit. Reduce the fruit to small
pieces in the liquidiser but do not purée. Mix the fruit with the
sugar and jelling agent and bring to the boil in a pan. Cook for
2 minutes at a rolling boil then pour into rinsed screw-top jars.
Stand the well-sealed jars upside down for 10 minutes. Then
allow to cool for at least 12 hours.

Preparation time: approx. 20 Min., per jar: approx. 2 g P, 1 g F, 33 g C, 153 kcal

TIP

You can replace the sugar with honey. To ensure the spread sets
well, cover the jars with a cloth while cooling. Do not move the
jars for at least 12 hours. Only then is the gelling process comple-
ted. The spread will keep in a cool and dark place for 8–10 months.

Carrot and Apple Spread

Cut **2 apples** in half, remove the cores and grate with skins on. Sprinkle with **2 tsp lemon juice**. Peel and grate **2 carrots**. Blend until smooth **150 g/5 oz cottage cheese**, the apple, the carrot and **50 ml/1½ fl oz stiffly-whipped cream** and season with **salt** and **pepper**. Sprinkle with **1 punnet of cress** and serve with fresh **wholemeal bread**.

Preparation time: approx. 15 Min., per serving: approx. 8 g P, 6 g F, 15 g C, 154 kcal

Apricot Spread

For 3–4 jars
Wash **500 g/1 lb 2 oz apricots**, remove the stones and purée the fruit.
Mix together **50 g/1¾ oz fruit purée, 3 tbsp maple syrup, 2 tsp agar-agar, 10 chopped lemon balm leaves** and the **juice of ½ a lemon**. Bring the remaining apricot purée to the boil and stir in the agar-agar mixture. Cook at a rolling boil for 2 minutes and then pour into rinsed screw-top jars. Leave the jars to cool.

Preparation time: approx. 20 Min., per jar: approx. 2 g P, 1 g F, 18 g C, 91 kcal

Mixed Fruit Salad

Mix together **225 ml/8 fl oz fruit juice** with **1 tbsp lime juice, 1 tbsp sugar, 1/2 tsp grated lime peel** and **1/2 tbsp cornflour**, bring to the boil in a pan while stirring, simmer for about 2 minutes and allow to thicken a little. Remove from the heat and leave to cool down somewhat. Mix together **100 g/3½ oz freshly skinned and diced pineapple, 100 g/3½ oz skinned banana in slices, 75 g/2½ oz diced honeydew melon, 2 skinned and diced kiwis** and **1 skinned, stoned and diced peach**. Pour the sauce over the fruit. Serve garnished with **mint leaves**.

Preparation time: approx. 20 Min., per serving: approx. 1 g P, 1 g F, 24 g C, 112 kcal

Melon Salad with Mint

Skin **1 honeydew melon** and **300 g/11 oz water melon**, remove the seeds and dice the flesh. Mix **400 g/14 oz mixed berries** (raspberries, bilberries, blackberries, blackcurrants) with the diced melon and leave to stand in a cool place for 30 minutes.

Blend to a purée **50 g/1¾ oz freshly chopped mint, 200 g/7 oz yoghurt** and **2 tbsp lemon juice** in the liquidiser. Season with a little **chilli powder** and **sugar**. Pour the sauce over the fruit.

Preparation time: approx. 25 Min., per serving: approx. 4 g P, 3 g F, 17 g C, 120 kcal

Crunchy Muesli

Mix **100 g/3¹/₂ oz crunchy breakfast flakes** and **4 tbsp chopped hazel-nuts** together in a bowl.

Rinse and drain **250 g/9 oz bilberries** and add to the flake mixture together with **1 tsp lemon juice**.

Divide the muesli between 4 bowls and pour about **125 ml/4 fl oz milk** into each bowl. Sweeten with **honey** if necessary.

Preparation time: approx. 10 Min., per serving: approx. 5 g P, 9 g F, 30 g C, 231 kcal

Wheat Muesli Basis Mixture

Mix together **100 g/3¹/₂ oz rolled oat flakes, 100 g/3¹/₂ oz wheat flakes, 60 g/2 oz chopped hazelnuts, 75 g/2¹/₂ oz linseed seeds, 75 g/2¹/₂ oz sesame seeds, 2 tbsp sunflower seeds** and **100 g/3¹/₂ oz raisins**, and mix according to taste with either **fruit, yoghurt, kefir** or **curd cheese**.
Fill screw-top jars with the basic mixture and store in a cool, dry place.

Preparation time: approx. 5 Min., per serving: approx. 14 g P, 20 g F, 50 g C, 438 kcal

Snacks
& Soups

Wild Herb Soup

Roast **4 tbsp crushed wholegrain barley** in a hot pan without fat for 3–4 minutes until they begin to release their aroma. Add **1 l/1³/₄ pints vegetable stock** and bring to the boil while stirring. Leave to swell for 5 minutes. Sweat **1 bunch wild herbs** (e.g. dandelion, sorrel, nettle tips, yarrow, wild garlic) in **2 tbsp heated butter** and fold into the soup. Season to taste with **salt, pepper** and **nutmeg**. Pour into bowls and add **1 tbsp stiffly-whipped cream** to each bowl.

Preparation time: approx. 20 min., per portion: approx. 1 g P, 6 g F, 4 g C, 80 kcal

Fresh Pea Soup with Cumin

Cook **200 g/7 oz fresh peas** in **500 ml/18 fl oz boiling vegetable stock** with **1 tsp ground cumin** for about 12 minutes. In the meantime, lightly fry **2 peeled and chopped onions** and **2 peeled and crushed cloves of garlic** in **2 tbsp heated olive oil** until translucent. Add **500 g/1 lb 2 oz diced tomatoes** and simmer for 10 minutes. Season with **salt, pepper** and **2 tbsp chopped basil**. Blend the peas in their cooking water to a purée, pour into bowls and top with the tomatoes. Garnish each bowl with a dollop of **crème fraîche**.

Preparation time: approx. 15 min., per portion: approx. 5 g P, 4 g F, 11 g C, 107 kcal

Stuffed Courgettes

Cut **4 cleaned and trimmed courgettes** into 5 cm/2 in pieces and scoop out the flesh. Fry **200 g/7 oz minced beef** in **1 tbsp hot olive oil** with **1 peeled and chopped clove of garlic** until crumbly, then season with **salt, pepper** and **1/2 tsp ground cumin**. Stir in **30 g/1 oz chopped pine kernels** and **1/2 bunch of chopped parsley** and use to stuff the courgettes. Place in a casserole dish and pour on **100 ml/3 1/2 fl oz white wine**. Top with **100 g/3 1/2 oz goat's cheese** log cut into slices and bake in the oven for 15–20 minutes at 200°C/390°F/Gas 6 (fan oven 180°C/355°F/Gas 4).

Preparation time: approx. 15 min.,

per portion: approx. 18 g P, 18 g F, 5 g C, 282 kcal

Stuffed Tomatoes

Cut off the tops of **12 tomatoes** to use as lids, carefully scoop out the seeds and juice. Season the tomatoes with **salt** and **pepper**. Stand upside down to drain.

Brown **190 g/6½ oz minced beef** in **3 tbsp heated olive oil**, remove from the pan. Mix **3 spring onions** cut into rings with the minced beef, **½ bunch of freshly chopped mint**, **1 tbsp lemon juice** and **3 tbsp olive oil** until the mixture is smooth.

Fill the tomatoes with the mixture, decorate with **mint leaves** and replace the tomato lids.

Preparation time: approx. 20 min., per portion: approx. 3 g P, 4 g F, 2 g C, 66 kcal

Chicory Rolls with Orange

4 heads of chicory · 8 slices mild, supple cheese · 1 tbsp
butter · 1 onion · 300 g/11 oz yoghurt · 8 tbsp white wine ·
1 orange · salt · pepper · cayenne pepper · nutmeg ·
1/2 bunch of freshly chopped herbs · 60 g/2 oz freshly grated
Parmesan

Clean the heads of chicory, remove the bitter, hard inner stem,
cut the heads in half and wrap with the cheese. Lay in a greased
casserole. Peel and finely chop the onion and mix with the
yoghurt, wine and the filleted and diced orange. Season the
mixture according to taste with the spices and herbs. Pour the
mixture over the chicory in the casserole and sprinkle with the
Parmesan. Bake in the oven for about 15 minutes at 190°C/
375°F/Gas 5 (fan oven 170°C/340°F/Gas 3).

Preparation time: approx. 15 min.,

per portion: approx. 22 g P, 24 g F, 10 g C, 367 kcal

TIP
Chicory contains so much vitamin A
that this dish alone provides over
50% of the daily requirement
of the vitamin.

Power Balls

Pour **125 ml/4 fl oz water** over 80 g/3 oz crushed wholegrain wheat and leave to swell. Purée **80 g/3 oz stoned dates** with **50 g/1¾ oz chopped almonds**. Drain the wheat grains, add to the date and almond mix together with **1 tbsp lemon juice** and **2 tbsp maple syrup** and work to a homogenous mass. Form around 20 balls from the mass and coat in **sesame** or **poppy seeds**.

Preparation time: approx. 10 min., per portion: approx. 1 g P, 1 g F, 6 g C, 46 kcal

Trout Tartar

Skin **4 smoked trout** and cut the flesh into small cubes.
Mix the diced trout together with **2 finely diced celery stalks,**
1/2 de-seeded and diced sweet red pepper and **1 diced gherkin**. Fold in
100 g/3 1/2 oz crème fraîche and season with **salt** and **pepper**. Butter
20 small pumpernickel rounds and top with the trout tartar. Garnish with
dill and serve.

Preparation time: approx. 20 min., per portion: approx. 27 g P, 13 g F, 8 g C, 258 kcal

Cream of Celeriac Soup with Oyster Mushrooms

Cook **300 g/11 oz peeled and chopped celeriac** for about 10 minutes in **800 ml/1½ pints heated vegetable stock**. Purée and season with **salt** and **pepper**. Fold **8 tbsp lightly whipped cream** into the soup. Wipe clean **200 g/7 oz trimmed oyster mushrooms** with a damp cloth and cut into pieces. Stir-fry in **4 tbsp vegetable oil** for 5 minutes. Season with **salt** and **pepper**. Add the mushrooms to the soup and serve garnished with **chive rings**.

Preparation time: approx. 20 min., per portion: approx. 3 g P, 11 g F, 12 g C, 125 kcal

Lettuce Soup with Salmon Strips

Sweat **1 peeled and chopped onion** in **1 tbsp hot butter**. Add and briefly braise **3 tbsp oat flakes**. Add **400 g/14 oz cleaned and chopped lettuce** and pour in **500 ml/18 fl oz vegetable stock**. Bring everything to the boil and season with **1 tsp lemon juice, 1 pinch of sugar, salt, pepper, cayenne pepper** and **nutmeg** according to taste. Purée the soup, reheat and fold in **60 ml/2 fl oz stiffly-whipped cream**. Add **100 g/3¹/₂ oz smoked salmon** cut into thin strips. Serve with **3 tbsp finely-chopped dill**.

Preparation time: approx. 20 min., per portion: approx. 7 g P, 9 g F, 6 g C, 136 kcal

Herb Drink

Finely chop **150 g/5 oz fresh spinach** and **1/2 bunch of chives, flat-leaf parsley** and **dill**. Stir together with **250 ml/9 fl oz soya milk, the juice of 1 lemon** and **300 ml/11 fl oz mineral water**. Blend everything to a purée. Season according to taste with **salt** and **pepper** and pour into 4 glasses.

Preparation time: approx. 15 min., per portion: approx. 11 g P, 6 g F, 3 g C, 126 kcal

Raw Kohlrabi with Apple

Arrange **2 peeled and thinly-sliced kohlrabi** on plates together with
3 cored apples cut into thin wedges. Sprinkle with the juice of **1 lemon**.
Stir together **300 g/11 oz low-fat curd cheese, the juice of ½ an orange,
salt, pepper, nutmeg** and **2 tbsp olive oil** and pour over the raw kohlrabi
and apple. Sprinkle with **2 tbsp chive rings**.

Preparation time: approx. 20 min., per portion: approx. 12 g P, 3 g F, 17 g C, 154 kcal

Oat-Flake Muesli Bar

For about 30 bars
150 g/5 oz dried fruit (e.g. apricots, prunes, figs, dates) ·
100 g/3½ oz butter · 3 tbsp honey · 70 g/2½ oz raisins ·
200 g/7 oz oat flakes · 50 g/1¾ oz chopped almonds ·
50 g/1¾ oz desiccated coconut · 100 g/3½ oz wholemeal
flour · 1 tsp baking powder

Pour hot water over the dried fruit and leave to swell. Place in a
sieve and allow to drain. Finely dice the dried fruit.
Place the butter and honey in a bowl and whisk until creamy.
Add the dried fruit, raisins, oat flakes, almonds, coconut, flour
and baking powder and mix everything together to a smooth
dough.
For each bar take 1 heaped tablespoon of dough and shape
it first of all to a ball then to a bar of 2 cm/¾ in width and
5 cm/2 in length. Place the bars on a baking tray lined with
baking paper.
Bake in the oven for about 20 minutes at 180°C/355°F/Gas 4
(fan oven 160°C/320°F/Gas 3). Place on a cake rack to cool.

Preparation time: approx. 20 min., per portion: approx. 2 g P, 5 g F, 11 g C, 103 kcal

TIP
These delicious muesli bars can also be
prepared with other dried fruit, such as
cherries, mangoes, papayas or melons.

Sandwich with Rocket

Mix together in a bowl **50 g/1¾ oz rich cream cheese, 100 g/3½ oz cottage cheese** and **50 g/1¾ oz crème fraîche**. Add **80 g/3 oz freshly grated Parmesan, 4 drained and chopped preserved sun-dried tomatoes, 2 tbsp stoned and chopped black olives** and **½ bunch of chopped parsley** and mix together well. Season with **salt** and **pepper**.
Spread the paste over **4 slices of sandwich bread** and top with **50 g/1¾ oz rocket**. Cover with another **4 slices of sandwich bread** and cut diagonally.

Preparation time: approx. 15 min., per portion: approx. 7 g P, 9 g F, 7 g C, 141 kcal

Chilled Cucumber Soup

Peel **1 cucumber**, cut in half, remove the seeds and cut into slices.
Mix together with **200 g/7 oz sour cream**, **250 ml/9 fl oz soured milk**
and **50 g/1¾ oz yoghurt**.
Add **2 spring onions** cut into rings and braised, the **juice of ½ a lemon** and
½ a chopped red chilli and finely purée everything. Season according to
taste with **salt** and stir in **2 tbsp finely chopped dill**. Briefly chill. Serve the
soup with **250 g/9 oz honeydew melon** scooped into balls.

Preparation time: approx. 20 min., per portion: approx. 5 g P, 5 g F, 10 g C, 143 kcal

Broccoli Soup with Croutons

Cook **1 kg/2 lb 4 oz broccoli florets** in **750 ml/1⅓ pints vegetable stock** for about 10 minutes. Then purée and season according to taste with **salt**, **pepper** and **nutmeg**. Remove the crusts from **2 slices of white bread**, dice and fry in **3 tbsp butter** until golden brown. Pour the soup into bowls and serve topped with **1 dollop crème fraîche** and **croutons**.

Preparation time: approx. 20 min.,
per portion: approx. 9 g P, 8 g F,
14 g C, 173 kcal

Gazpacho

Peel **800 g/1 lb 12 oz tomatoes**, remove the seeds and dice. Peel **2 onions, 2 garlic cloves** and **1 cucumber**. Remove the seeds from **2 green peppers**. Dice ½ a pepper as well as the cucumber and 1 onion. Purée the tomatoes with the remaining onion, garlic and the rest of the peppers. Add **2 slices of white bread** with the crusts removed, **5 tbsp olive oil** and **3 tbsp sherry vinegar**, and purée once again. Season according to taste with **salt** and **pepper**. Pour the soup into bowls and sprinkle with the diced vegetables.

Preparation time: approx. 30 min., per portion: approx. 4 g P, 7 g F, 16 g C, 157 kcal

Scones with Fillet of Trout

For 20 scones

Prepare a dough using **175 g/6 oz flour, 1½ tsp baking powder, 1 pinch of salt, 50 g/1¾ oz softened butter** and **1 egg**. Gradually add up to **3 tbsp cream** until the dough acquires a sleek gloss. Roll out the dough on a floured surface until about 2 cm/¾ in thick and cut out rounds. Lay the scones on a baking tray lined with baking paper and bake in the oven for about 10 minutes at 200°C/390°F/Gas 6 (fan oven 180°C/355°F/Gas 4). Leave to cool covered with a cloth. Cut the scones in half and spread with **150 g/5 oz sour cream** mixed with ¾ tbsp freshly grated horseradish and **2 tbsp freshly chopped dill**. Cut 175 g/6 oz fillet of trout into 20 pieces. Cover each scone with one piece. Decorate with **dill, tartar sauce, creamed horseradish** or **caviar**.

Preparation time: approx. 25 min.,
per portion: approx.
3 g P, 4 g F, 6 g C,
78 kcal

Fish Curry

Cut **500 g/1 lb 2 oz skinned sea bass fillets** into bite-sized pieces and marinate in **2 tbsp oyster sauce** and **4 tbsp fish sauce** for about 30 minutes. Heat **4 tbsp vegetable oil** in a wok, roast **1 tbsp palm sugar** and **1 tbsp red curry paste** in the oil, pour in **800 ml/1 pint 8 fl oz coconut milk** and bring to the boil. Add **1 sliced courgette** and simmer for about 5 minutes. Drain **400 g/14 oz tinned lychees**, stir into the curry sauce, add the fish pieces and simmer everything together for a further 2 minutes. Serve decorated with **1 red chilli** cut into rings.

Preparation time: approx. 15 min., per portion: approx. 25 g P, 13 g F, 24 g C, 318 kcal

Fresh Vegetable Soup

Peel **2 cucumbers**, cut in half, remove the seeds and dice.
Remove the seeds and dice **2 green peppers**, peel and dice **2 carrots** and
cut **3 celery sticks** into small pieces. Clean and chop **4 spring onions**.
Purée all the ingredients in a liquidiser and mix together with **300 ml/
11 fl oz tomato juice** and **50 ml/1 ¾ fl oz olive oil**. Season with **salt,
pepper** and **Tabasco sauce** according to taste. Serve with fried **croutons**.

Preparation time: approx. 20 min., per portion: approx. 5 g P, 13 g F, 14 g C, 208 kcal

Green Spelt Grain Soup

Roast **70 g/2½ oz crushed unripe spelt grain** in a pan without fat. Pour in **1 l/1¾ pints vegetable stock**, bring to the boil and season with **salt, pepper** and **nutmeg**. Whisk together **1 egg yolk** and **2 tbsp crème fraîche** and stir into the soup. Finely grate **2 peeled carrots** and add to the soup. Simmer for 3 minutes. Serve sprinkled with **2 tbsp freshly chopped parsley**.

Preparation time: approx. 10 min., per portion: approx. 4 g P, 7 g F, 14 g C, 140 kcal

Artichoke Hearts in Tomato Sauce

800 g/1 lb 12 oz tomatoes · 3 tbsp olive oil · 1 garlic clove · 4 tbsp tomato purée · salt · pepper · 16 artichoke hearts from a jar · 1 tbsp freshly chopped chervil

Scald the tomatoes, peel, remove the stalk cores and seeds and dice the flesh. Heat the oil in a pan. Peel the garlic, finely chop and sweat in the hot oil. Add the diced tomatoes and mash together. Stir in the tomato purée and season with salt and pepper. Drain the artichoke hearts, add to the tomato sauce, cover and simmer for about 10 minutes. Reduce the sauce until thick and creamy and serve sprinkled with chervil and accompanied by fresh wholemeal bread rolls.

Preparation time: approx. 20 min., per portion: approx. 3 g P, 4 g F, 7 g C, 84 kcal

TIP
Artichokes are not only delicious, they are also very healthy. They contain a lot of potassium, magnesium, folic acid and vitamin C.

Sorrel Soup

Finely chop **150 g/5 oz sorrel**, setting a few leaves aside for later. Peel and finely dice **1 onion**. Lightly fry the onion and sorrel in **2 tbsp melted butter**, dust with **1 tbsp flour** and sweat the mixture while stirring. Pour in **1 l/ 1³/₄ pints stock,** simmer for 20 minutes then purée the soup.

Whip **200 ml/7 fl oz cream** until stiff and cut the reserved sorrel leaves into thin strips. Remove the soup from the heat, stir in **1 egg yolk** then fold in the whipped cream. Season with **salt** and **pepper** according to taste and garnish with the strips of sorrel.

Preparation time: approx. 10 min., per portion: approx. 11 g P, 25 g F, 6 g C, 295 kcal

Artichokes with Herbal Dip

Wash **4 large artichokes**, remove the stalks and cut off the leaf tips with scissors. Cook for about 25 minutes in plenty of boiling salted water seasoned with **the juice of 1 lemon**. Meanwhile, mix together **200 g/7 oz yoghurt, 100 g/3¹/₂ oz reduced fat crème fraîche** and **100 ml/3¹/₂ fl oz cream**. Stir in **3 small chopped green pepperonis** from a jar, **5 chopped stoned black olives**, **1 bunch of chopped mixed spring herbs** and **1 peeled and chopped garlic clove** as well as **1 tsp mustard**, then season the dip with **salt** and **pepper** according to taste. Drain the artichokes. Pluck off the leaves, dipping the fleshy part in the sauce.

Preparation time: approx. 10 min., per portion: approx. 7 g P, 26 g F, 12 g C, 322 kcal

Tomato Soup

Skin **1 kg/2 lb 4 oz tomatoes**, remove the seeds and dice the flesh. Heat **3 tbsp oil** in a pan and lightly fry **1 chopped onion**. Add the diced tomato, **2 celery sticks** chopped in pieces and **1 bay leaf** and braise together. Pour in **150 ml/5 fl oz vegetable stock** and bring to the boil.

Simmer the tomato soup for about 30 minutes until the vegetables are tender. Then purée and season with **salt**, **pepper** and **Tabasco sauce** according to taste. Serve sprinkled with **chopped basil**.

Preparation time: approx. 30 min., per portion: approx. 3 g P, 4 g F, 9 g C, 95 kcal

Asparagus Soup with Salmon

Peel **600 g/1 lb 5 oz white asparagus**, trim the ends and cut the spears into pieces of 3 cm/1 in length. Put the tips to one side. Cook the asparagus pieces in **1 l/1¾ pints chicken stock** until al dente.

Fry **200 g/7 oz salmon fillet** cut into strips in **2 tbsp oil**, remove and drain on kitchen towel. Purée the asparagus pieces in the stock and refine the soup with **100 ml/3½ fl oz cream**. Season with **salt, pepper** and **nutmeg**. Add the asparagus tips and allow them to heat through in the soup for 5 minutes. Season according to taste with **lemon juice**. Add the salmon strips and serve garnished with **2 spring onions** cut into rings.

Preparation time: approx. 30 min., per portion: approx. 17 g P, 15 g F, 9 g C, 233 kcal

Stuffed Lettuce Rolls

60 g/2 oz Italian mortadella • 10 black olives without
stones • 50 g/1 3/4 oz sheep's milk cheese • salt • pepper •
1/2 bunch basil • 8 large leaves cos lettuce (or 16 small ones) •
2 tbsp olive oil

Cut the mortadella into strips. Chop the olives, cut the sheep's
milk cheese into cubes. Mix with the olives and mortadella strips,
season with salt and pepper. Pluck the basil leaves from the
stems and finely chop. Mix together with the filling mixture. Rinse
the lettuce leaves, pat dry and lay out on a work surface. Lay out
overlapping if using small leaves. Spread the filling over the lettuce leaves, roll up and secure with toothpicks. Heat up the olive
oil and gently fry the lettuce rolls on all sides at low temperature
for about 5 minutes.

Preparation time: approx. 20 min., per portion: approx. 6 g P, 24 g F, 3 g C, 257 kcal

TIP

Other leaf vegetables can be used to make these rolls,
for example chard, Savoy cabbage or Chinese leaves.
Briefly blanch Savoy cabbage, white cabbage and red
cabbage leaves in boiling water before filling.

Vegetable Kebabs

Prepare a marinade using **75 ml/2½ fl oz olive oil, 1 peeled and chopped garlic clove, 1 tsp mustard, 2 tbsp chopped Mediterranean herbs** and **salt** and **pepper**. Alternately thread onto 8 skewers **1 red and 1 yellow sweet pepper** cut into chunks, **2 courgettes** cut into 2 cm/³/₄ in slices, **1 aubergine** cut into chunks and **2 peeled onions** cut into eighths, and steep them in the marinade for 15 minutes. Then grill the skewers for about 10 minutes. Serve with **wholemeal baguette.**

Preparation time: approx. 10 min., per portion: approx. 4 g P, 13 g F, 15 g C, 201 kcal

Cucumber Relish

For about 2 250 ml/9 fl oz jars
Peel **4 cucumbers**, purée and mix with **4 cleaned and finely cut spring onions, 1 bunch of chopped dill** and **5 tbsp salt**. Leave to stand for 20 minutes and then place in a muslin cloth and squeeze out thoroughly. Mix **2 cm/³/₄ in peeled and grated ginger, 250 ml/9 fl oz white wine vinegar, 3 mustard seeds** and **a little pepper** with the cucumber purée and use to fill screw-top jars. Use within 10 weeks. Serve with **bread** and **herb curd cheese**.

Preparation time: approx. 20 min.,
per jar: approx. 5 g P,
1 g F, 20 g C, 138 kcal

Tortilla with Vegetables

Cut **1 green pepper** into strips, peel **1 large onion** and cut into rings. Remove the stalk cores from **300 g/11 oz tomatoes** and cut into eighths. Peel and finely grate **2 small potatoes**. Heat up **3 tbsp olive oil** and gently fry the onion and green pepper. Add the potato, braise together for 3 minutes, then fold in the tomatoes. Whisk together **8 eggs, 1 bunch of chopped flat-leaf parsley** and **100 ml/3½ fl oz vegetable stock**, season with **salt** and **pepper,** and pour over the vegetables. Cover with a lid and allow to set for about 8 minutes. Cut into 4 portions and serve while still hot.

Preparation time: approx. 15 min., per portion: approx. 18 g P, 17 g F, 12 g C, 280 kcal

Toast Sandwich with Turkey and Herb Curd Cheese

Mix together **1 bunch chives** cut into rings, **100 g/3¹/₂ oz curd cheese (20% fat), 1 tbsp medium-hot mustard, salt** and **pepper**.
Toast **8 slices wholemeal bread** and spread thinly with the curd cheese mixture. Lay **4 slices smoked turkey breast** on 4 slices of toast and top with **2 slices of peeled cucumber**. Cover with the remaining 4 slices of toast and cut the sandwiches in half diagonally.

Preparation time: approx. 10 min., per portion: approx. 8 g P, 3 g F, 21 g C, 153 kcal

Prawn Balls

For 15 balls

Mix together **3 de-seeded and finely chopped chillies**, **3 spring onions** cut into rings, **1 chopped garlic clove** and **3 cm/1 in peeled and grated ginger**. Purée 2/3 of the chilli mixture together with **¹/₂ bunch coriander**, **3 kaffir lime leaves** and **1 tbsp fish sauce**, add **125 g/4¹/₂ oz fish fillet** and stir until creamy. Fold in **125 g/4¹/₂ oz cooked prawn meat**. Allow **15 g/¹/₂ oz glass noodles** to soften in hot water. Cut into small pieces and stir into the mixture.

Form small balls out of the mixture and fry them until golden brown in **1 tbsp hot peanut oil**. Prepare a dip from the remaining chilli, spring onion, garlic and grated ginger mixture and **125 ml/4 fl oz rice vinegar, 1 tbsp fish sauce** and **1 tbsp brown sugar**, and serve with the prawn balls.

Preparation time: approx. 30 min.,
per portion: approx. 4 g P, 1 g F, 1 g C, 34 kcal

100

Puff Pastry with Tuna

For 8 pasties

Lightly roll out the defrosted individual sheets of **300 g/11 oz frozen puff pastry** and sprinkle with water. Out of each sheet cut 2 rounds of pastry (about 12 cm/5 in diameter).

Drain **a tin of tuna**, loosen up the fish with a fork, mix together with **1 finely chopped sweet red pepper** with the seeds removed and **1/2 bunch of finely chopped parsley**. Season with **salt, pepper** and **1/2 tsp sweet paprika powder**.

Whisk **1 egg yolk** with **a little water** and use to brush the pastry edges. Place 2 tbsp filling on one half of each pastry round, fold the other half over and press down the pastry edge to seal. Bake in the oven for about 20 minutes at 200°C/390°F/Gas 6 (fan oven 180°C/355°F/Gas 4).

Preparation time: approx. 20 min., per portion: approx. 6 g P, 16 g F, 11 g C, 218 kcal

Smoked Salmon Pockets on Salad

Roll **12 slices of smoked salmon** around a filling made from **200 g/ 7 oz ricotta**, **150 g/5 oz sour cream**, **1/2 tsp grated lemon peel**, **2 tbsp lemon juice**, **¹/₂ bunch of chopped chervil, dill and chives, salt** and **pepper**. Draw the edges together and tie with **chives**.
Arrange **120 g/4 oz lamb's lettuce** and the leaves of **¹/₄ Chinese cabbage** cut into strips on plates.
Mix together **1 tbsp white wine vinegar, the grated peel and juice of 1 orange, 4 tbsp walnut oil** and **salt** and **pepper**, and pour over the salad. Top with the salmon pockets and serve.

Preparation time: approx. 30 min. , per portion: approx. 21 g P, 17 g F, 7 g C, 270 kcal

Pumpkin Soup

Gently fry **1 peeled and chopped onion** in **1 tbsp hot butter**. Add **500 g/ 1 lb 2 oz diced Hokkaido pumpkin** with the seeds removed and **2 peeled and diced carrots**, and continue to cook. Pour in **1 l/1³/4 pints vegetable stock**, bring to the boil and simmer for about 15 minutes. Finally, purée the soup and season with **salt, pepper, nutmeg** and **ground ginger** according to taste. Serve garnished with **toasted almond flakes** and **crème fraîche**.

Preparation time: approx. 15 min., per portion: approx. 5 g P, 17 g F, 10 g C, 222 kcal

Salmon Bagels

For 4 bagels

Slice open **4 sesame bagels** and toast until golden. Mix **1 bunch of chopped dill** with **150 g/5 oz cream cheese**. Spread the cream cheese over the bottom half of each bagel and cover with **2 slices of salmon**. Top with **thin slices of onion** and the top half of the bagel.

Preparation time: approx. 15 min., per portion: approx. 7 g P, 12 g F, 24 g C, 240 kcal

Potato and Vegetable Hash Browns

For 6–8 fritters
Grate **4 medium-sized peeled potatoes, 2 scraped carrots, 1 trimmed courgette, 2 peeled onions** and **50 g/1³/₄ oz peeled celeriac** and season with **salt, pepper** and **1 tsp thyme**. Form 6-8 fritters from the mixture and fry in **3 tbsp hot butter** until crisp and golden brown. Serve with a sauce made from **250 g/9 oz yoghurt, 4 tbsp crème fraîche, salt, pepper, 1 chopped onion** and **1 chopped garlic clove**.

Preparation time: approx. 30 min., per fritter: approx. 4 g P, 3 g F, 19 g C, 130 kcal

Melon with Vinaigrette

1 small cantaloupe melon • $1/2$ cucumber • 3 tomatoes •
salt • 3 tbsp freshly chopped mint • 3 tbsp olive oil •
2 tbsp white balsamic vinegar • $1/2$ tsp ground cumin •
mint to garnish

Cut the melon in half, scoop out the seeds, and remove the flesh
with a melon baller. Peel and dice the cucumber. Skin the tomatoes, remove the seeds and dice. Mix the melon balls and diced
cucumber and tomato in a bowl together with salt and 2 tbsp
mint. Leave to steep for 10 minutes.
Prepare a vinaigrette using oil, vinegar, the remaining mint,
cumin and salt and sprinkle over the salad mixture. Allow
everything to steep for a further 30 minutes. Serve the salad
garnished with mint.

Preparation time: approx. 20 min., per portion: approx. 1 g P, 4 g F, 5 g C, 64 kcal

TIP

You can always tell if a melon is ripe by the smell.
If it smells fruity it is ripe. The skin should be firm
and unyielding when pressed.

Buttermilk Pumpkin Muffins

For 12 muffins

Mix together **280 g/10 oz flour, 1¹/₂ tsp bicarbonate of soda, ¹/₂ tsp salt** and **50 g/1³/₄ oz sugar**. Whisk together **100 g/3¹/₂ oz butter, 1 egg, 75 g/2¹/₂ oz sugar** and **250 ml/9 fl oz buttermilk** until foamy, then fold in **1 peeled, cored and grated apple** and **100 g/3¹/₂ oz grated pumpkin**. Mix with the flour mixture to make a smooth dough. Divide the mixture between 12 paper cases in a muffin tray and bake in the oven for about 20 minutes at 170°C/340ºF/Gas 3 (fan oven 150°C/300ºF/Gas 2). Leave to stand for 5 minutes then remove. Sprinkle with **cinnamon** and decorate with **apple** and **pumpkin wedges**.

Preparation time: approx. 25 min., per muffin: approx. 3 g P, 7 g F, 29 g C, 205 kcal

Herb Muffins with Cream Cheese

For 12 muffins

Mix **2 eggs, 120 ml/4 fl oz rapeseed oil, 200 g/7 oz yoghurt** and **1/2 tsp salt** to a smooth mass.

Mix **200 g/7 oz each of wholemeal wheat flour** and **white wheat flour** with **2 tsp baking powder** and **1 tsp bicarbonate of soda** and add to the egg mixture together with **25 g/1 oz frozen mixed herbs**.

Place 12 paper cake cases in a muffin tray add fill with about 2/3 of the mixture. Add **1 tsp herb cream cheese** to each muffin then top with the remaining mixture. Bake in the oven for about 25 minutes at 180°C/355°F/ Gas 4 (fan oven 160°C/320°F/Gas 3).

Preparation time: approx. 20 min., per portion: approx. 5 g P, 12 g F, 22 g C, 223 kcal

Spelt Fritters

Add **200 g/7 oz crushed unripe spelt grain** to 400 ml/14 fl oz boiling **vegetable stock**, bring back to the boil, remove from the heat and leave to swell for 10 minutes.

Heat **1 tbsp rapeseed oil** in a pan, add **1 chopped onion, 1 chopped garlic clove** and **1 leek** cut into fine rings, and gently braise while stirring.

Mix the vegetables, the unripe spelt, **2 eggs**, **½ tsp curry powder, salt** and **pepper** to a smooth mass.

Shape 8 fritters from the mixture and fry on all sides in **2 tbsp rapeseed oil** until crisp.

Preparation time: approx. 20 min., per portion: approx. 5 g P, 3 g F, 17 g C, 127 kcal

Toast Wedges with Lentil Paste

Lightly braise **75 g/2¹/₂ oz red lentils** and **1 crushed garlic clove** in **1 tbsp hot olive oil**. Pour in **200 ml/7 fl oz vegetable stock** and simmer everything for about 15 minutes. Drain the lentils well, then purée together with **2 tbsp olive oil**. Mix the purée with **1 tbsp tomato purée, 2 tbsp grated Parmesan, ¹/₂ bunch of chopped basil, salt** and **pepper**. Spread the lentil paste over **8 slices of toasted bread.** Top half the slices with **50 g/1³/₄ oz well-drained young spinach**, cover with the other slices of toast and cut in half diagonally.

Preparation time: approx. 15 min.,
per portion: approx. 4 g P, 3 g F, 17 g C, 123 kcal

Salads

Kohlrabi Salad with Tomatoes

Cut **500 g/1 lb 2 oz peeled kohlrabi** first into eighths, then into slices. Finely chop the leaves. Skin **3 tomatoes**, remove the stalk cores and seeds and cut into wedges. Mix together **2 tbsp wine vinegar** with **1 tbsp orange juice**, **½ tsp salt, pepper, 4 tbsp oil** and **1 tbsp freshly chopped parsley**. Pour the dressing over the vegetables and leave to stand for 15 minutes.

Preparation time: approx. 20 min., per portion: approx. 3 g P, 5 g F, 7 g C, 89 kcal

Curly Endive Salad with Nuts

Mix together 1/2 **head rinsed curly endive lettuce, 80 g/3 oz cooked red lentils** and **100 g/3**1/2 **oz rinsed radish sprouts.** Roast **3 tbsp freshly chopped walnuts** and **1 tbsp chopped hazelnuts** in a pan.
Prepare a dressing with **1 tbsp red wine vinegar,** 1/2 **tsp mustard, 3 tbsp olive oil, 2 chopped shallots, salt** and **pepper** and mix with the curly endive, lentils and radish sprouts. Fold in the nuts. Serve the salad accompanied by **freshly toasted garlic bread.**

Preparation time: approx. 20 min.,

per portion: approx. 4 g P, 7 g F,

13 g C, 137 kcal

Asparagus Salad

Cut **750 g/1 lb 10 oz peeled white asparagus** into chunks and cook in lightly salted boiling water for 12–15 minutes. Remove and drain. Peel **2 hard-boiled eggs** and finely dice, slice **4 radishes** and **4 spring onions** into thin rings. Mix all the salad ingredients together in a bowl and toss in a dressing made from **2 tbsp white wine vinegar, 3 tbsp sunflower oil, 1 tsp fig mustard, salt** and **pepper**. Serve sprinkled with **2 tbsp freshly chopped parsley.**

Preparation time: approx. 30 min., per portion: approx. 9 g P, 7 g F, 9 g C, 145 kcal

Green Asparagus Salad with Parsnips

Cut **100 g/3¹/₂ oz peeled parsnips** into thin sticks and blanch for 3 minutes. Cut **200 g/7 oz prepared green asparagus** in half and cook in boiling salted water for about 5 minutes. Drain the vegetables. Gently fry **8 peeled and chopped shallots** in **2 tbsp soya oil** for about 4 minutes.

Shred **6–8 lollo rosso leaves** and place on 4 plates. Top with the asparagus chunks, parsnips and shallots. Prepare a dressing from **4 tbsp white wine vinegar, 4 tbsp soya oil, 1 tsp mustard, salt** and **pepper** and sprinkle over the salad. Serve garnished with **lemon wedges**.

Preparation time: approx. 20 min.,

per portion: approx. 2 g P, 5 g F, 6 g C, 94 kcal

Salad with Brussels Sprouts

Cook **500 g/1 lb 2 oz cleaned and trimmed Brussels sprouts** in **500 ml/ 1 pint vegetable stock** for about 10 minutes until al dente. Remove the sprouts, drain, place in a bowl and put the stock to one side. Cut **2 peeled carrots** and **200 g/7 oz peeled celeriac** into thin sticks, blanch both in the vegetable stock and then add to the bowl with the sprouts. Clean and trim **2 spring onions**, slice into rings and also add to the bowl. Season **200 g/ 7 oz herbal crème fraîche** with **salt, pepper, 2 tbsp lemon juice** and **nutmeg** and pour over the vegetables.

Preparation time: approx. 25 min., per portion: approx. 9 g P, 18 g F, 12 g C, 253 kcal

Carrot and Pear Salad with Honey Dressing

Cut **500 g/1 lb 2 oz peeled carrots** into slices and blanch in boiling salted water for 2 minutes. Remove and allow to drain. Clean, trim and remove the seeds from **1 green pepper**, peel and remove the core from **1 pear**, dice both, and add to the carrots. Stir in **3 tbsp rinsed raisins**. Mix together **the juice of 1 lemon, 3 tbsp safflower oil, 2 tsp honey, 150 g/5 oz yoghurt, salt** and **pepper** and pour over the salad. Serve garnished with **2 tbsp freshly chopped chervil**.

Preparation time: approx. 30 min., per portion: approx. 3 g P, 6 g F, 13 g C, 121 kcal

Couscous Salad

200 g/7 oz couscous · 3 tomatoes · 1 bunch spring onions ·
1 green pepper · 1 red chilli · 1 courgette · 1 bunch flat-leaf
parsley · 1/2 bunch coriander · 3 tbsp lime juice · 5 tbsp
olive oil · salt · pepper · 150 g/5 oz sour cream · 1 tsp cumin

Prepare the couscous according to the instructions on the packet.
Remove the stalk cores from the tomatoes and dice. Slice the
spring onions into rings. Remove the seeds from the pepper and
the chilli, dice both, and also dice the courgette. Rinse, shake dry
and finely chop the herbs. Mix all the ingredients with the lime
juice and olive oil. Fold in the couscous and season. Mix the sour
cream with the cumin and salt and serve with the couscous salad.

Preparation time: approx. 20 min.,

per portion: approx. 5 g P, 10 g F, 23 g C, 210 kcal

TIP
You can also prepare this salad with millet or
rice instead of couscous. Fried strips of meat
can also be mixed in if you prefer.

Green Bean Salad with Coconut

Blanch **225 g/8 oz trimmed green beans** in boiling salted water for about 5 minutes, drain, rinse in cold water and cut into small pieces. Mix with **1 chopped green pepperoncini** and **1 chopped red pepperoncini** and arrange on top of **radicchio leaves**. Roast **3 tbsp desiccated coconut** in a wok and put onto a plate.

Gently fry **6 garlic cloves** cut into thin slices in **100 ml/3½ fl oz heated peanut oil** until golden yellow. Drain on kitchen towel. Add the coconut and garlic to the beans. Prepare a dressing with **50 ml/1¾ fl oz lime juice, 50 ml/1¾ fl oz coconut milk, 1 tbsp chilli paste, 1 tbsp oyster sauce** and **1 tbsp sugar** and pour over the salad. Serve garnished with **3 tbsp freshly chopped coriander**.

Preparation time: approx. 35 min.,
per portion: approx. 2 g P, 27 g F, 8 g C, 280 kcal

Lentil Salad with Spinach

Cook **250 g/9 oz red lentils** according to the directions on the packet and drain well. When cooled down, mix with **3 tbsp vegetable stock, 1 pinch cayenne pepper** and **½ tsp dried thyme**. Mix **200 g/7 oz prepared spinach leaves** with **1 peeled, cored and diced apple**. Mix together **2 tbsp apple vinegar, 2 tbsp cream, 2 tbsp safflower oil, salt** and **pepper** and pour over the spinach and apple. Season the lentils with **1 tbsp balsamic vinegar, salt** and **pepper** and serve with the spinach and apple salad.

Preparation time: approx. 35 min., per portion: approx. 16 g P, 5 g F, 36 g C, 253 kcal

Lamb's Lettuce with Tofu

Cook **1 celeriac root** in boiling water for 20 minutes. Peel and grate when cooled down. Sort, rinse and shake dry **300 g/11 oz lamb's lettuce**. Fry **150 g/5 oz smoked tofu** in **2 tbsp hot olive oil** until crisp. Heat up **200 ml/ 7 fl oz vegetable stock** and when slightly cooled stir in **3 tbsp raspberry vinegar**. Arrange the salad on plates and coat with the dressing.

Preparation time: approx. 30 min., per portion: approx. 8 g P, 7 g F, 1 g C, 103 kcal

Fried Tofu
on Spinach Salad

Prepare a marinade from **4 tbsp soy sauce, 2 tbsp lemon juice, herbal salt, 1/4 tsp cayenne pepper** and **pepper** and use to marinate **250 g/9 oz tofu** cut into cubes for 15 minutes. Then coat the cubes with **50 g/1³/4 oz flour** and fry in **3 tbsp heated olive oil** until crisp. Place **150 g/5 oz prepared wet spinach leaves** into a pan and while stirring cook for 5 minutes until they collapse. Remove and drain. Season the tofu marinade with **the juice of 1 lemon** and mix together with the spinach. Arrange the drained tofu cubes on top of the spinach and serve garnished with **spring onions** sliced into rings and **1/2 bunch of finely chopped chives**.

Preparation time: approx. 20 min., per portion: approx. 12 g P, 10 g F, 7 g C, 178 kcal

Fennel Salad with Fresh Figs

Remove the outer skin from **2 fennel bulbs**, cut in half, then slice thinly. Remove the skin from **3 figs** with a peeler then cut into strips. Mix together the fennel and figs. Prepare a dressing with **1 peeled, cored and grated apple, 2 chopped walnuts, 75 g/ 2½ oz sour cream, 1 tbsp lime juice, 1 tsp tomato ketchup, salt, pepper** and **2 tbsp rapeseed oil** and pour over the salad. Garnish with **chopped dill**.

Preparation time: approx. 20 min., per portion: approx. 3 g P, 7 g F, 6 g C, 112 kcal

Watercress Salad
with Sunflower Seeds

Remove the cores from **2 peeled pears** and dice. Prepare a dressing by blending the fruit to a purée together with **200 g/7 oz yoghurt, the juice of 1 lemon, salt, pepper, 1 pinch of sugar** and **4 tbsp walnut oil**. Clean and sort **2 bunches of watercress** (about 150 g/5 oz) and pluck the leaves from the stems. Peel **2 more pears**, remove the cores and cut into thin strips. Mix with the watercress and coat with the dressing. Serve the salad sprinkled with **60 g/2 oz roasted sunflower seeds**.

Preparation time: approx. 15 min., per portion: approx. 6 g P, 14 g F, 14 g C, 212 kcal

Cucumber Salad Royal

4 eggs · 1 generous pinch of tamarind powder · 1 small onion · 2 garlic cloves · 1 piece fresh ginger (2–3 cm/ 3/4–1 in) · 3 sprigs of coriander · 1 stick lemon grass · 1 tsp shrimp paste · 1 tsp sugar · salt · 1/2 tsp cumin · pepper · 3 1/2 tsp turmeric powder · 300 ml/11 fl oz coconut milk · 1 cucumber · 200 g/7 oz cooked prawns · 1/2 bunch coriander

Hard boil the eggs. Mix the tamarind powder with 1 tbsp water and leave to swell. Place the chopped onion, the chopped garlic, the peeled and chopped ginger, the chopped coriander and the peeled and chopped lemon grass in a wok.
Mix together well the shrimp paste, sugar, salt, cumin, pepper, tamarind paste and turmeric and also add to the wok. Pour in the coconut milk. Bring everything to the boil while stirring, remove from the heat and leave to cool.
Thinly slice the cucumber. Shell the eggs and cut in half. Arrange the cucumber, eggs, prawns and coriander leaves on plates and coat with the seasoned sauce.

Preparation time: approx. 30 min., per portion: approx. 9 g P, 9 g F, 9 g C, 139 kcal

TIP
Turmeric is a spice that stains with an intensive colour. A kitchen apron should therefore be worn when using it.

Salad with Sheep's Cheese and Beetroot

Cook **6 cleaned and trimmed beetroots** in boiling water for about 30 minutes. Drain, allow to cool then peel and cut into slices. Mix together with **3 tbsp balsamic vinegar, 2 tbsp mustard** and **1 tsp coarsely-ground black pepper** and leave to steep for 1 hour.

Mix **150 g/5 oz each of both lamb's lettuce** and **rocket** with **200 g/ 7 oz sheep's cheese** cut into cubes and **1 bunch of freshly chopped mint**. Sprinkle with **5 tbsp olive oil**, mix together well and season with salt. Top with the slices of beetroot.

Preparation time: approx. 20 min., per portion: approx. 11 g P, 16 g F, 6 g C, 212 kcal

Rocket Salad with Potato and Egg

Arrange **400 g/14 oz washed rocket leaves** on plates. Peel **250 g/ 9 oz boiled potatoes**, dice and add to the leaves. Bring to the boil **4 chopped shallots** in **125 ml/4 fl oz vegetable stock**, leave to cool down. Season with **salt** and **pepper** and pour over the salad. Braise **1 onion** sliced into rings and **50 g/1¾ oz diced lean bacon** in **2 tbsp butter**. Spread over the salad. Top with **2 diced hard-boiled eggs**.

Preparation time: approx. 30 min., per portion: approx. 10 g P, 8 g F, 12 g C, 160 kcal

Indian Salad with Apple

Cut into strips **150 g/5 oz cleaned and trimmed white cabbage, 250 g/9 oz peeled carrots** and **50 g/1¾ oz celery**. Mix together with **2 peeled, cored and finely diced apples**. Fold in **3 tbsp rinsed raisins** and **2 tbsp chopped almonds**. Prepare a dressing by mixing together **5 tbsp sunflower, the juice of ½ lemon, 4 tbsp cream, salt** and **a pinch of curry powder** and stir into the salad. Fold in **4 tbsp radish sprouts**.

Preparation time: approx. 20 min., per portion:
approx. 3 g P, 8 g F, 14 g C, 136 kcal

Asparagus Salad with Apple

Cut **800 g/1 lb 12 oz cleaned, trimmed and peeled green asparagus** into 3 cm/1 in pieces and boil for 5 minutes in boiling salted water with **a little sugar**. Remove and allow to drain. Slice **3 peeled and cored apples** into thin wedges and arrange on plates together with the cooled pieces of asparagus.

Mix together **3 tbsp orange juice, 3 tbsp salad mayonnaise, 150 g/ 5 oz sour cream** and **2 tsp sweet mustard**, season according to taste with **salt, pepper** and **sugar**, and pour over the salad. Serve sprinkled with **chopped chervil**.

Preparation time: approx. 25 min.,
per portion: approx. 6 g P, 8 g F, 17 g C, 161 kcal

Dressed Asparagus with Strips of Trout

1 kg/2 lb 4 oz green asparagus · 1 tsp salt · 1 tsp sugar ·
200 g/7 oz smoked fillet of trout · 3 tbsp lemon juice ·
4 tbsp walnut oil · pepper · 1/2 bunch dill

Clean and trim the asparagus, peel the bottom third and cut into
pieces. Cook for 10 minutes until al dente in 1 l/1³/₄ pints boiling water and season with 1/2 tsp each of salt and sugar. Pour off
the water, drain the asparagus and place in a bowl to cool down.
Cut the trout fillets into thin strips. Mix together the lemon juice,
walnut oil, remaining salt and sugar, pepper and chopped dill
and pour over the asparagus. Fold in the strips of trout and allow
the salad to steep for about 30 minutes.

Preparation time: approx. 30 min., per portion: approx. 16 g P, 7 g F, 6 g C, 155 kcal

TIP
You can replace the trout with cooked
chicken breast. Cut the breast into strips
and serve with the asparagus.

Lettuce Leaves with Oyster Mushrooms and Olives

Tear **1 cleaned and trimmed oak-leaf lettuce** and **1 cleaned and trimmed radicchio** into bite-sized pieces and arrange on plates. Sweat **2 peeled and chopped shallots** together with **2 peeled and chopped garlic cloves** in **3 tbsp sunflower oil** until translucent. Gently fry together with **600 g/21 oz cleaned, trimmed and finely cut oyster mushrooms** for 3 minutes. Season according to taste with **salt** and **pepper**. Cut **4 tomatoes** into quarters and place on top. Prepare a dressing with **8 tbsp red wine vinegar, 1 tsp mustard, 8 tbsp olive oil, salt** and **pepper** and dribble over the salad. Serve sprinkled with **100 g/ 3¹/₂ oz sliced black olives** and **1 bunch of freshly chopped chervil.**

Preparation time:
approx. 30 min., per portion:
approx. 6 g P, 18 g F, 6 g C, 214 kcal

136

Kohlrabi Salad with Walnut Dressing

Blanch **3 peeled kohlrabi** cut into strips in **500 ml/18 fl oz boiling vegeta-ble stock** for 3 minutes, remove, drain and allow to cool. Add to the kohlrabi **1 bunch of chopped basil, 1 tbsp chopped lemon balm leaves** and **1 peeled and grated carrot**. Toss in a dressing prepared with **100 ml/ 3½ fl oz cream, 2 tbsp lemon juice, 1 tbsp walnut oil, salt** and **pepper**. Serve sprinkled with **2 tbsp chopped walnuts**.

Preparation time: approx. 20 min., per portion: approx. 4 g P, 13 g F, 8 g C, 168 kcal

Avocado Salad with Mushrooms

Remove the skins and stones from **2 ripe avocados** and cut into thin slices. Drizzle with **the juice of 1 lime**. Mix a dressing with **6 tbsp white wine vinegar, salt, pepper, 1 pinch of dried oregano** and **4 tbsp walnut oil** and pour half over the avocados. Cover with aluminium foil and place in the fridge to marinate for 30 minutes. Sprinkle **100 g/ 3¹/₂ oz sliced mushrooms** with **2 tbsp lime juice**, cut **100 g/3¹/₂ oz cherry tomatoes** in half, mix both with **1 peeled and chopped shallot** and add the remaining dressing. Arrange on plates topped with the avocado slices.

Preparation time:

approx. 15 min., per portion:

approx. 3 g P, 32 g F, 2 g C, 302 kcal

Lamb's Lettuce with Mushrooms

Sprinkle **1 tbsp lemon juice** over **200 g/7 oz cleaned and halved brown mushrooms** and, while stirring, fry gently in **1 tbsp hot butter** for 2 minutes. Season with **salt** and **pepper**. Stir in **½ bunch of chopped parsley** and **1 peeled and crushed garlic clove**. Mix together in a bowl **150 g/5 oz cleaned and sorted lamb's lettuce** with a dressing prepared with **2 tbsp raspberry vinegar, 4 tbsp sunflower oil, salt** and **pepper**. Arrange on plates and top with **2 tbsp roasted pumpkin seeds** and the mushrooms.

Preparation time: approx. 15 min.,
per portion: approx. 2 g P,
8 g F, 1 g C, 98 kcal

139

Cauliflower and Broccoli Salad

Cook **400 g/14 oz each of both broccoli** and **cauliflower florets** in a covered pan containing **300 ml/11 fl oz boiling vegetable stock** for about 7 minutes until al dente. Drain and allow to cool. Clean and trim **1/2 bunch spring onions** and slice into thin rings. Finely chop **1 peeled hard-boiled egg.** Mix together **150 g/5 oz yoghurt, 50 g/ 1³/4 oz crème fraîche, 2 tbsp fruit vinegar** and **1 tsp curry powder** and season according to taste with **salt, pepper** and **sugar**. Mix the cauliflower and broccoli with the sauce and onion rings. Garnish with the egg and **1/2 bunch of chopped chives**.

Preparation time: approx. 25 min.,
per portion: approx. 10 g P, 9 g F, 10 g C, 164 kcal

Celeriac and Endive Salad

Blanch **300 g/11 oz endive lettuce** cut into strips and **100 g/3¹/₂ oz peeled celeriac** cut into sticks for 1 minute in boiling salted water, and mix together with **3 tbsp mung bean sprouts**. Cut in half **1 pear**, remove the core and thinly slice. Arrange the salad on plates and top with the pear slices. Prepare a dressing with **the juice of ¹/₂ an orange, 100 g/3¹/₂ oz soured milk, 1 generous pinch ground ginger, salt** and **pepper** and pour over the salad.

Preparation time: approx. 25 min., per portion: approx. 3 g P, 1 g F, 8 g C, 56 kcal

Buckwheat Salad with Sweet Corn

Strip the corn from **4 fresh cobs of sweet corn**, cook in boiling salted water for about 6 minutes until al dente, rinse in cold water and drain. Arrange **100 g/3½ oz cleaned and sorted lamb's lettuce** on plates. Prepare a dressing with **3 tbsp balsamic vinegar, 1 tsp lime juice, 10 tbsp rapeseed oil, 2 tbsp vegetable stock, salt** and **pepper** and drizzle over the lamb's lettuce. Top with the drained sweet corn and **50 g/1¾ oz buckwheat** and serve garnished with **2 diced hard-boiled eggs** and **1 bunch of chopped chives**.

Preparation time: approx. 30 min.,
per portion: approx. 9 g P, 17 g F, 25 g C, 293 kcal

Pea Sprout Salad with Tomatoes and Sheep's Cheese

Gently fry **200 g/7 oz washed pea sprouts** in **2 tbsp hot butter** for about 2 minutes. Season with **herbal salt, pepper** and **1 tsp dried marjoram** and leave to cool. Mix together the pea sprouts, **250 g/9 oz diced tomatoes** with the stalk cores removed and **1 chopped onion** and crumble **50 g/ 1³/₄ oz sheep's cheese** on top. Stir together **4 tbsp white wine vinegar** and **3 tbsp sunflower oil** and pour over the salad. Serve sprinkled with **2 tbsp basil** cut into strips.

Preparation time: approx. 20 min.,

per portion: approx. 6 g P, 9 g F, 5 g C, 127 kcal

Warm Vegetable Salad

650 g/1 lb 8 oz Chinese cabbage • salt • 4 onions • 2 garlic cloves • 7 tbsp sesame oil • 200 g/7 oz each of tinned palm hearts and bamboo shoots • 125 ml/4 fl oz vegetable stock • 200 g/7 oz radish • 2 nori sheets • 8 tbsp soy sauce • 6 tbsp lemon juice • 8 tbsp sweet rice wine • 5 tbsp vegetable stock • 1 tbsp five-spice powder

Cut the cleaned and trimmed Chinese cabbage into strips, blanch for 3 minutes in boiling salted water and drain. Dice the onions and crush the garlic. Sweat the onion and garlic in 4 tbsp heated oil. Cut the drained palm hearts and bamboo shoots into small pieces and add to the onions.
Pour in the vegetable stock and add the peeled and diced radish. Toast the nori sheets. Mix together the soy sauce, lemon juice, rice wine, remaining sesame oil, vegetable stock and five-spice powder and season with salt and pepper according to taste. Add the Chinese cabbage to the vegetables in the pan and heat through. Arrange everything on plates and drizzle with the sauce. Tear the nori sheets into small pieces and sprinkle over the salad.

Preparation time: approx. 30 min.,

per portion: approx. 5 g P, 13 g F, 10 g C, 184 kcal

TIP

This warm vegetable salad becomes a complete meal when served with sticky rice. If you wish, you can also stir in roasted peanuts.

Fitness Salad

Cut **200 g/7 oz endive lettuce** into fine strips, cut **1 bunch radishes** into slices. Blanch **200 g/7 oz mung bean sprouts** in boiling water then drain. Place the ingredients in a bowl and mix together with **4 tbsp roasted sunflower seeds** and **1/2 bunch of chopped parsley** and **chives**.
Prepare a dressing with **4 tbsp herb vinegar, 6 tbsp rapeseed oil, salt** and **pepper** and pour over the salad. Serve with a **fresh baguette**.

Preparation time: approx. 15 min., per portion: approx. 5 g P, 12 g F, 3 g C, 152 kcal

Lamb's Lettuce with Celeriac and Ham

Mix together **150 g/5 oz cleaned and sorted lamb's lettuce** and **200 g/ 7 oz peeled and grated celeriac**. Cut **100 g/3 ½ oz air-dried ham** into strips. Prepare a dressing with **4 tbsp raspberry vinegar, 6 tbsp olive oil, salt** and **pepper** and pour over the salad. Fold in the strips of ham. Sprinkle with **20 g/¾ oz roasted sunflower seeds**.

Preparation time: approx. 20 min., per portion: approx. 2 g P, 10 g F, 2 g C, 126 kcal

147

Green Spelt Grain Salad with Apple

Soak **125 g/4½ oz unripe spelt grains** overnight in water, boil in the soaking water for about 45 minutes and allow to swell. Cut **300 g/11 oz cleaned and trimmed fennel** into fine strips. Grate **2 peeled and cored apples** and sprinkle with **2 tbsp lemon juice**. Mix **50 g/1¾ oz Roquefort cheese** together with **50 g/1¾ oz cottage cheese, 1 tbsp Calvados, 60 ml/ 4 tbsp milk, salt** and **pepper** and mix with the spelt grains, fennel and apple. Serve topped with **2 tbsp chopped chives**.

Preparation time: approx. 20 min., per portion: approx. 10 g P, 6 g F, 31 g C, 226 kcal

Colourful Millet Salad

Sweat **1 diced onion** in **1 tbsp hot butter**. Add **200 g/7 oz millet**, cook for about 20 minutes in **500 ml/18 fl oz vegetable stock** and allow to cool. Mix the millet with **1/2 peeled and diced cucumber**, **250 g/9 oz tomatoes** cut into wedges and **1 head of frisée lettuce** torn into small pieces. Prepare a dressing with **200 g/7 oz yoghurt, 2 tbsp oil, 2 tbsp tomato ketchup, 1 tbsp cider vinegar, salt, pepper** and **2 tbsp chopped chives** and pour over the salad. Mix everything together thoroughly.

Preparation time: approx. 25 min., per portion: approx. 10 g P, 10 g F, 42 g C, 300 kcal

Warm Mushroom Salad with Goat's Cheese

Cook **375 g/13 oz cleaned, trimmed and peeled green asparagus** in boiling water for about 5 minutes, drain and rinse in iced water. Toss **200 g/ 7 oz rinsed and trimmed lettuce leaves** in a sauce made from **1 tbsp chopped shallots, 1 chopped garlic clove, 3 tbsp olive oil, 1 tbsp tarragon mustard, 2 tbsp raspberry vinegar, salt** and **pepper**. Arrange on plates with the asparagus and **125 g/4½ oz goat's cheese** cut into slices. Sweat **375 g/13 oz cleaned mushrooms** together with **1 chopped shallot** and **1 chopped garlic clove** in **1 tbsp olive oil** until soft. Season and place on top of the salad while still warm. Serve sprinkled with **2 tbsp chopped chives**.

Preparation time: approx. 30 min., per portion: approx. 14 g P, 9 g F, 4 g C, 155 kcal

Lollo Rosso with Quail Eggs

Clean
and rinse
**1 head lollo
rosso**, shake
dry, tear the
leaves into
pieces and arrange
on plates. Top with
3 shallots cut into rings and
8 drained and diced artichokes from a
jar. Prepare a dressing with
**100 ml/3½ fl oz vegetable
stock, 1 tsp mustard,
3 tbsp sherry vinegar,
3 tbsp safflower oil,
salt, pepper** and **sugar**
according to taste, and
drizzle over the salad. Arrange
16 cherry tomatoes cut in half and
**8 boiled, peeled and halved
quail
eggs** on
top and
serve
sprinkled
with **1 hand-
ful of cress**.

Preparation time: approx. 30 min.,
per portion: approx. 13 g P, 9 g F, 7 g C, 166 kcal

Sweet Peppers and Tomato Salad

2 green peppers · 1 yellow pepper · 3 large tomatoes ·
1 garlic clove · 1 tbsp sherry vinegar · 5 tbsp olive oil ·
$^1/_2$ tsp sugar · salt · pepper · $^1/_2$ bunch coriander

Preheat the oven to 200°C/390°F/Gas 6 (fan oven 180°C/
355°F/Gas 4). Clean the peppers, cut in half and remove the
seeds. Lay them on a baking tray with the cut surface facing the
tray, and bake in the oven until the skin blackens. Remove from
the oven, allow to cool, skin and cut into pieces.
Skin the tomatoes, remove the stalk core and seeds and cut the
flesh into 2 cm/$^3/_4$ in chunks. Crush the garlic.
Place the peppers and tomatoes in a bowl. Mix a dressing using
the garlic, vinegar, oil, sugar, salt and pepper and pour over the
salad. Decorate with coriander leaves and serve.

Preparation time: approx. 45 min., per portion: approx. 2 g P, 7 g F, 7 g C, 103 kcal

TIP
Instead of skinning the peppers through the more time
consuming procedure of baking, you could skin them
with a potato peeler. However, If you do, the peppers
will not have a roasted flavour.

Celery and Grape Salad

Cut **300 g/11 oz celery** into thin strips. Mix together with **150 g/5 oz black grapes** with the seeds removed and cut in half and **30 g/1 oz roasted pumpkin seeds**. Prepare a dressing with **1 bunch of chopped dill, 100g/ 3 ¹/₂ oz yoghurt, 2 tbsp lemon juice, herbal salt, pepper, ¹/₂ tsp sweet paprika powder** and **a pinch of sugar** and mix with the salad. Serve sprinkled with **2 tbsp cress**.

Preparation time: approx. 20 min., per portion: approx. 4 g P, 5 g F, 11 g C, 109 kcal

Radish Salad with Cress

Soak **50 g/1¾ oz spelt** for 12 hours then boil in the soaking water for about 30 minutes until soft. Grate **400 g/14 oz peeled radish** and mix together with the cooked spelt grains, **1 tbsp lemon juice, 1 tsp honey, 8 walnut kernels, 1 handful cress, 100 g/3½ oz crème fraîche, salt** and **pepper.**

Preparation time: approx. 25 min., per portion: approx. 8 g P, 21 g F, 15 g C, 280 kcal

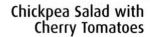

Chickpea Salad with Cherry Tomatoes

Place in a bowl **450 g/1 lb drained chickpeas** from a tin, **225 g/8 oz cherry tomatoes** cut in half and **1 chopped shallot**. Stir together **1 crushed garlic clove, 2 tbsp olive oil, 1 tbsp lemon juice, salt** and **pepper** and mix with the vegetables. Allow to stand overnight, then serve garnished with **2 tbsp chopped parsley**.

**Preparation time: approx. 20 min.,
per portion: approx. 6 g P, 5 g F, 18 g C, 140 kcal**

Bean Sprout Salad

Thoroughly rinse **500 g/1 lb 2 oz bean sprouts** and allow to drain. Blanch in boiling salted water for 1 minute, remove, rinse in cold water and drain well. Place in a bowl and mix together with a dressing prepared from **2 tbsp light soy sauce, 1 tbsp rice wine vinegar, 2 tbsp sesame oil** and **salt**. Slice **2 spring onions** into rings and fold into the salad.

Preparation time: approx. 15 min., per portion: approx. 8 g P, 5 g F, 7 g C, 101 kcal

Grain Salad with Vegetables

Soak **100 g/3¹/₂ oz wheat grains** overnight, drain and then cook in **500 ml/18 fl oz boiling vegetable stock** for about 30 minutes. After 18 minutes add **100 g/3¹/₂ oz rinsed red lentils** to the grains. Clean and trim **250 g/9 oz celery** and **¹/₂ bunch spring onions** and finely dice. Gently fry in **1 tbsp hot oil**. Pour in **4 tbsp herb vinegar** and season with **salt, pepper** and **a little sugar**. Stir in **5 tbsp soya oil**. Mix everything together with the cooled wheat grains and lentils and leave to stand for 30 minutes. Arrange and serve on **lettuce leaves**.

Preparation time: approx. 30 min.,
per portion: approx. 10 g P, 11 g F, 31 g C, 260 kcal

Sweet Corn, Tomato and Cucumber Salad

Mix together **4 diced tomatoes, 1 peeled and sliced cucumber, 4 tbsp fresh boiled sweet corn** and **3 spring onions** sliced into rings. Fold in **½ bunch of freshly chopped herbs.**
Mix together **4 tbsp wheat germ oil, 3 tbsp herbal vinegar, salt, pepper** and **½ tsp garlic powder** and pour over the salad. Serve sprinkled with **2 tbsp chopped green olives**.

Preparation time: approx. 20 min., per portion: approx. 1 g P, 6 g F, 6 g C, 83 kcal

Vegetable Salad with Preserved Lemon

3 green peppers • 2 aubergines • 2 eggs • 1 tbsp fruit vinegar • salt • 150 ml/5 fl oz vegetable oil • 1/2 preserved lemon • 150 g/5 oz green olives without stones • 2 tbsp olive oil • juice of 1 lemon • pepper • 1 tbsp freshly chopped parsley

Preheat the oven to 180°C/355ºF/Gas 4 (fan oven 160°C/320ºF/Gas 3). Bake the peppers in the oven for 20 minutes until the skin blackens and blisters. Remove from the oven, allow to cool, skin, remove the seeds and cut the peppers into pieces. Cut the cleaned and trimmed aubergines into chunks of roughly 1 cm/1/3 in. Separate the egg yolks from the whites, whisk the whites and mix with vinegar and 1/2 tsp salt. Coat the aubergine chunks in this mixture and fry in hot oil. Remove from the pan and leave to drain. Peel the preserved lemon, rinse the peel, dry and finely dice. Mix the vegetables with the lemon peel and olives. Stir together a dressing using the olive oil, lemon juice, salt and pepper and pour over the salad. Serve sprinkled with parsley.

Preparation time: approx. 45 min., per portion: approx. 7 g P, 24 g F, 9 g C, 280 kcal

TIP
To prepare preserved lemons take 1 kg/2 lb 4 oz lemons and cut 5 slits lengthways in each lemon and stuff with 250 g/9 oz coarse salt. Place in a container, scald with boiling water, cover with oil and allow to stand for 3 minutes.

Tomato and Egg Salad

Skin **500 g/1 lb 2 oz tomatoes**, remove the stalk cores and seeds, and then dice. Mix together in a bowl the tomatoes, **1 chopped onion, 1 bunch of finely chopped chives** and **4 hard-boiled eggs**. Stir together **the juice of 1 lemon, 3 tbsp sunflower oil, mustard, salt** and **pepper** and pour over the salad. Serve garnished with **1 boiled egg** cut into wedges and **2 tbsp freshly chopped chervil.**

Preparation time: approx. 30 min.,
per portion: approx. 12 g P, 13 g F,
8 g C, 197 kcal

Spring Salad with Mozzarella

Mix together **200 g/7 oz rinsed and sorted mixed lettuce leaves, 2 spring onions in rings, 1 trimmed red pepper** with the seeds removed and cut into strips, **4 diced tomatoes** and **1 peeled avocado** cut into slices. Sprinkle with **lemon juice**. Slice **200 g/7 oz mozzarella** and add to the salad. Mix together **6 tbsp olive oil, 2 tbsp balsamic vinegar, 2 tbsp freshly chopped basil, salt** and **pepper** and pour over the salad.

Preparation time: approx. 25 min., per portion: approx. 13 g P, 31 g F, 7 g C, 363 kcal

Greek Pumpkin Salad

400 g/14 oz pumpkin · 1 large onion · 1 green und 1 red
pepper · 3 mild green pepperoncini · 2 tomatoes · 2 garlic
cloves · 5 tbsp olive oil · 100 ml/3^1/2 fl oz vegetable stock ·
1 tbsp lemon juice · 1 tbsp white wine vinegar · salt · pepper ·
2 tbsp chopped parsley · black olives according to taste

Peel the pumpkin, remove the seeds and inner fibres, cut the flesh
into chunks. Chop the onion. Trim the peppers, remove the seeds
and cut into strips. Trim the pepperoncini, remove the seeds and
slice into thin rings. Remove the stalk cores from the tomatoes
and cut into slices. Chop the garlic.
Gently fry the diced pumpkin in 2 tbsp hot oil, pour in the vegetable stock and braise for about 5 minutes so that the pumpkin
remains al dente. Leave to cool.
Mix a dressing from the lemon juice, vinegar, remaining oil, salt
and pepper. Place the pumpkin in a bowl together with the rest
of the vegetables, the garlic and the dressing and mix. Fold in
the parsley and garnish according to taste with olives.

Preparation time: approx. 40 min., per portion: approx. 3 g P, 11 g F, 10 g C, 155 kcal

TIP

For this delicious pumpkin salad choose a
variety with a fine nutty flavour, for example
a Hokkaido pumpkin or a butternut squash.

Lamb's Lettuce with Cranberry Vinaigrette

Mix **1 head radicchio** cut into strips with **150 g/5 oz cleaned and sorted lamb's lettuce** and **3 peeled, cored and diced apples**. Prepare a dressing with **1 chopped shallot, 4 tbsp cider vinegar, salt, pepper, 1 tsp sugar, 4 tbsp sunflower oil** and **3 tbsp cranberry sauce**.
Pour over the salad. Serve with **fresh toast**.

Preparation time: approx. 15 min., per portion: approx. 2 g P, 6 g F, 17 g C, 131 kcal

Endive Lettuce with Radishes

Cut **1 head rinsed and sorted endive lettuce** into strips, mix with **1 bunch of sliced radishes, 4 spring onions sliced into rings, 50 g/1³/₄ oz chopped stuffed olives** and **1 tbsp chopped capers**. Prepare a dressing with **1 hard-boiled egg yolk** passed through a sieve, **1 tsp mustard, salt, pepper, 3 tbsp white wine vinegar, 4 tbsp olive oil** and **2 tbsp cream**. Mix the ingredients of the salad with the dressing and leave to stand for 5 minutes before serving.

Preparation time: approx. 20 min., per portion: approx. 2 g P, 15 g F, 5 g C, 165 kcal

Leek Salad with Curd Cheese Dressing

Thoroughly wash **350 g/12 oz leeks,** trim and drain. Remove the dark green leaves and slice the leeks into thin rings. To make the dressing mix **50 g/ 2 oz cream curd cheese** with **1 tsp oil, 4 tbsp milk, 1 tbsp white wine vinegar, salt** and **pepper** and pour over the leeks. Sprinkle **1 tbsp chopped dill** and **1 tbsp chopped hazelnuts** on top and serve.

Preparation time: approx. 15 min.,
per portion: approx. 4 g P, 2 g F,
4 g C, 56 kcal

Spinach Salad with Lentils

Drain **200 g/7 oz tinned cooked brown lentils** and mix with **3 tbsp vegetable stock, 1 pinch cayenne pepper** and **1 tsp chopped thyme**. Mix Together **200 g/7 oz rinsed and sorted spinach** with **1/2 peeled celeriac root** cut into sticks and thoroughly coat with a sauce made from **2 tbsp white wine vinegar, 2 tbsp cream, salt, pepper** and **3 tbsp sunflower oil**. Mix the lentils with **1 diced tomato, 1 tbsp balsamic vinegar** and **salt** and serve with the salad.

Preparation time: approx. 20 min., per portion: approx. 14 g P, 4 g F, 27 g C, 206 kcal

Cos Lettuce with Tomatoes and Olives

Cut **1 head cleaned and trimmed cos lettuce** into 3 cm/1 in strips and mix with **500 g/1 lb 2 oz skinned and diced plum tomatoes** with the seeds removed, **150 g/5 oz sliced green olives stuffed with almonds** and **1 large onion** cut into thin rings.
Prepare a dressing by stirring together **2 tbsp crème fraîche, 1 tsp mustard, 2 tbsp red wine vinegar, salt, pepper, 2 tbsp olive oil** and **2 tbsp safflower oil** and mix with the salad.

Preparation time: approx. 30 min., per portion: approx. 5 g P, 16 g F, 6 g C, 187 kcal

Mixed Lettuce Salad with Lime Dressing

Mix together **150 g/5 oz yoghurt, 2 tbsp mustard, 2 cleaned and trimmed spring onions** sliced into rings, **4 tbsp cider vinegar** and **the juice of 2 limes**. Season with **salt, pepper** and **cayenne pepper**. Tear up into small pieces **1 head of oak-leaf lettuce, 1 head of cos lettuce** and **½ a head of radicchio** and mix with the dressing. Dry-roast **8 tbsp mixed seeds** and sprinkle over the salad.

Preparation time: approx. 20 min., per portion: approx. 2 g P, 3 g F, 4 g C, 66 kcal

Colourful Appetizer Salad

Cook **100 g/3¹/₂ oz cleaned, trimmed and finely cut green beans** in boiling salted water for 5–7 minutes. When cooled, mix with **10 cherry tomatoes** cut in half and **100 g/3¹/₂ oz drained tinned sweet corn**. Mix together **1 tbsp balsamic vinegar, 1 tbsp sherry vinegar, 2 tbsp sunflower oil, salt** and **pepper** and pour over the salad. Lay **125 g/4¹/₂ oz cooked sliced turkey breast** over the arranged salad. Serve topped with **2 boiled eggs** cut into wedges and sprinkled with **2 tbsp freshly chopped chervil**.

Preparation time: approx. 30 min., per portion: approx. 17 g P, 12 g F, 21 g C, 265 kcal

Radicchio Salad with Mushrooms

Clean and trim **2 heads of radicchio**, tear the leaves into small pieces.
Sprinkle **400 g/14 oz sliced mushrooms** with some of a marinade prepared
from **the juice of 1–2 lemons, 4 tbsp walnut oil, 1 crushed garlic clove,
1 bunch of chopped chervil, salt** and **pepper** and leave to stand for
15 minutes. Then mix with the remaining marinade and the radicchio.

Preparation time: approx. 20 min., per portion: approx. 4 g P, 6 g F, 6 g C, 100 kcal

Rocket Salad with Fried Halloumi

Arrange on plates **600 g/1 lb 5 oz cleaned, sorted and chopped rocket leaves** and **150 g/5 oz cherry tomatoes** cut in half. Sprinkle with **2 tbsp flaked almonds** and **2 tbsp chopped chives**. Mix together **125 ml/ 4 fl oz grape juice**, **$\frac{1}{2}$ tsp mustard**, **2 tbsp fruit vinegar**, **2 tbsp soya oil**, **salt** and **pepper** and pour over the salad. Cut **200 g/7 oz halloumi** into cubes, fry until crisp in **2 tbsp olive oil** and arrange on top of the salad.

Preparation time: approx. 30 min., per portion: approx. 9 g P, 9 g F, 88 g C, 158 kcal

Artichoke Salad with Ham

Mix **250 g/9 oz drained and quartered artichoke hearts** from a tin or jar with **4 fresh tomatoes** cut into eighths, **25 g/1 oz drained sun-dried tomatoes** cut into strips, **25 g/1 oz stoned black olives** cut in half and **50 g/2 oz Parma ham** cut into strips. Mix together **2 tbsp herb vinegar, 3 tbsp olive oil, 1 crushed garlic clove, 1/2 tsp mustard, salt, pepper** and **sugar** according to taste and pour over the salad. Serve sprinkled with **1 tbsp freshly chopped basil**.

Preparation time: approx. 20 min., per portion: approx. 6 g P, 7 g F, 6 g C, 114 kcal

Fruity Chicory Salad

2 heads chicory · 400 g/14 oz green grapes · 1 mango ·
1/2 honeydew melon · 100 g/3 1/2 oz dried dates · 250 ml/
9 fl oz buttermilk · 5 tbsp grappa · 2 tbsp double cream ·
3 tbsp mango juice · lemon pepper · 1 pinch each of both
ground cardamom and ground cloves · 50 g/1 3/4 oz chopped
pecan nuts · flowers to garnish

Cut the chicory in half, remove the bitter core and slice the leaves
into strips. Cut the grapes in half and remove the seeds. Peel the
mango, cut in half then cut the fruit away from the stone in
wedges. Remove the seeds from the melon then cut out the flesh
using a melon baller. Remove the stones from the dates and cut
the fruit into strips. Mix the fruit and chicory together in a bowl.
Mix the buttermilk with the grappa, the double cream and the
mango juice and season with the spices. Pour over the salad and
serve garnished with the pecan nuts and flowers.

Preparation time: approx. 30 min., per portion: approx. 6 g P, 11 g F, 44 g C, 305 kcal

TIP
You can mix 250 g/9 oz boiled rice into this
fruity salad to create a delicious festive dish
that will enrich any party buffet.

Radish Salad

Grate **2 large peeled radishes** into thin slices, salt and leave to stand for around 10 minutes. Mix together **2 tbsp sour cream, 150 g/5 oz yoghurt, 2 tbsp lemon juice, pepper** and **1 pinch of sugar**. Thinly slice **2 peeled and cored apples** and **½ cucumber** cut in half and with the seeds removed. Mix the drained radish with the apple, cucumber and salad dressing. Serve garnished with **1 bunch of chopped dill**.

Preparation time: approx. 30 min., per portion: approx. 3 g P, 2 g F, 12 g C, 84 kcal

Broccoli Salad with Sesame

Cook **400 g/14 oz broccoli florets** in boiling salted water for about 4 minutes. Drain and rinse in cold water. When fully drained mix together with **2 chopped shallots, 100 g/3½ oz cherry tomatoes** cut in half, **2 hard-boiled and diced eggs** and **1 bunch chives** sliced into rings. Prepare a dressing with **3 tbsp sherry vinegar, 1 tsp mustard, salt, pepper** and **4 tbsp safflower oil** and mix with the salad. Dry-roast without oil **2 tbsp sesame seeds** and sprinkle over the salad.

Preparation time: approx. 20 min., per portion:

approx. 8 g P, 10 g F, 4 g C, 164 kcal

Courgette Salad with Cashew Nuts

4 courgettes (about 800 g/1¾ lb) · salt · pepper · 10 tbsp
olive oil · 4 tomatoes · 2 spring onions · 1 bunch thyme ·
100 g/3½ oz cashew nuts · 1 head radicchio · 4 tbsp
balsamic vinegar

Clean, trim and cut the courgettes into slices. Season with salt and
pepper. Briefly fry in 3 tbsp hot oil. Then remove from the pan
and drain. Skin the tomatoes, remove the stalk cores and seeds,
and dice the flesh. Clean and trim the spring onions and slice into
rings. Chop the thyme, setting a few leaves aside for later.
Roast the cashew nuts in a pan without oil. Arrange the cleaned
and sorted radicchio leaves on plates. Top with the sliced courgettes, diced tomatoes and spring onion rings. Prepare a dressing
with the thyme, the remaining olive oil, balsamic vinegar, salt
and pepper and pour over the salad. Sprinkle with the cashew
nuts. Serve garnished with the thyme leaves and accompanied
with garlic baguette.

Preparation time: approx. 30 min., per portion: approx. 9 g P, 24 g F, 16 g C, 315 kcal

TIP
Cashew nuts contain less fat than all other nuts.
In addition, 75 % of the fat they contain consists
of valuable unsaturated fatty acids.

Tunisian Salad

Mix **2 cleaned, trimmed, de-seeded and diced green peppers** together with **¹/₂ peeled and diced cucumber, 6 chopped spring onions** and **4 diced tomatoes**. Add **200 g/7 oz drained tinned chickpeas**. Mix together **1 bunch of chopped coriander, 6 tbsp lemon juice, 4 tbsp olive oil, salt** and **pepper** and pour over the salad.

Preparation time: approx. 20 min., per portion: approx. 5 g P, 7 g F, 18 g C, 154 kcal

Dandelion Salad with Egg and Mustard Dressing

Rinse and sort **400 g/14 oz dandelion leaves** and tear into small pieces. Mix with **1 chopped shallot** and **½ bunch of chopped mixed herbs**. Pass **the yolks of 2 hard-boiled eggs** through a sieve and mix together with **1 tbsp herb mustard, 6 tbsp safflower oil, salt, pepper** and **sugar** according to taste. Pour over the salad. Dice the egg whites and sprinkle over the salad together with **1 chopped shallot** and the remaining herbs.

Preparation time: approx. 35 min., per portion: approx. 7 g P, 12 g F, 10 g C, 173 kcal

Vegetarian

Braised Winter Vegetables

Gently fry **2 peeled and chopped shallots** in **2 tbsp hot butter** until translucent.

Add **250 g/9 oz peeled and diced carrots, 1 leek cut into rings, 200 g/7 oz celery cut into rings** and **100 g/3½ oz white cabbage** cut into strips and gently sauté. Add **5 tbsp vegetable stock** and simmer everything together for about 10 minutes. Blend together **1 tsp arrowroot flour** and **150 ml/¼ pint vegetable stock** until smooth and add to the vegetables. Mix together **100 g/3½ oz crème fraîche, 1 tbsp drained capers, 1 pinch paprika, salt, pepper** and **nutmeg** and stir into the pan. Serve garnished with **2 tbsp chopped coriander.** Freshly-baked bread tastes delicious with this dish.

Preparation time: approx. 20 min., per portion: approx. 3 g P, 11 g F, 7 g C, 147 kcal

Pointed Cabbage Fritters with Radish Sauce

Boil **400 g/14 oz peeled and diced potatoes** in a little salted water for about 10 minutes, drain and purée. Cut **1 cleaned and trimmed pointed cabbage** (about 400 g/14 oz) into strips, cook in **150 ml/¼ pint vegetable stock** for about 10 minutes and drain. Work to a dough with the **potato purée, 3 tbsp oat flakes, 2 tbsp potato starch** and **2 egg yolks**. Mix together with **salt, pepper, ½ tsp curry powder** and **1 tbsp chopped parsley**. Coat about 12 fritters in **50 g/1¾ oz breadcrumbs** and fry in **3 tbsp hot oil**. Mix **1 bunch radishes** cut into slices with **2 tbsp hot vegetable stock** and **150 g/5 oz each of both sour cream and yoghurt**, season with **salt** and **pepper**. Serve with the fritters.

Preparation time: approx. 20 min., per portion: approx. 11 g P, 14 g F, 39 g C, 337 kcal

Vegetables Hot Pot with Sunflower Sprouts

Gently fry **1 peeled and chopped onion** in **3 tbsp heated butter.**
Add **500 g/1 lb 2 oz scraped and sliced carrots** as well as **400 g/
14 oz peeled and diced potatoes** and simmer while stirring. Add **4 tbsp
vegetable stock**, season with **salt** and **pepper** and cook with the lid on for
about 7 minutes. Fold in **300 g/11 oz prepared spinach** in strips and allow
to collapse. Season according to taste with **nutmeg**. Stir in **150 g/
5 oz crème fraîche,** then fold **6 tbsp sunflower sprouts** into the vegetables
in the pan.

Preparation time: approx. 25 min., per portion: approx. 6 g P, 18 g F, 21 g C, 282 kcal

188

Pointed Cabbage with Lemon Yoghurt Sauce

Cut **800 g/1 lb 12 oz pointed cabbage** into eighths, remove the hard core and sauté in **2 tbsp hot butter** for 2 minutes. Pour in **125 ml/4 fl oz vegetable stock** and simmer the cabbage in it for about 15 minutes. Remove and keep warm. Blend **350 g/12 oz cream yoghurt** with **1 tsp flour,** mix with the cooking stock and bring to the boil. Add **the juice and grated peel of 1 untreated lemon** and season according to taste with **salt** and **pepper**. Arrange and serve the cabbage coated with the sauce.

Preparation time: approx. 15 min., per portion: approx. 7 g P, 10 g F, 17 g C, 197 kcal

Fried Fennel with Pomegranate

2 bulbs fennel · 4 tbsp olive oil · 4 tbsp lime juice · 2 tsp
honey · salt · pepper · 1 pinch cumin · 400 g/14 oz carrots ·
1 pomegranate

Clean and trim the fennel, cut in half, remove the hard core, and
thinly slice the bulbs lengthways. Mix together 2 tbsp oil, the
lime juice, the honey and the spices. Heat the remaining olive oil
and fry the fennel slices in it until they start to brown. Arrange
on plates and sprinkle with some of the lime marinade. Peel and
grate the carrots, mix with the remaining marinade. Arrange on
top of the fennel. Cut open the pomegranate, scoop out the
seeds and sprinkle over the fennel and carrots.

Preparation time: approx. 25 min., per portion: approx. 3 g P, 5 g F, 11 g C, 112 kcal

TIP

As an alternative, you could brush the fennel slices
with oil and place under a hot grill.

Courgette in Herb Marinade

Cut **4 courgettes** into slices, dab dry, season with **salt** and **pepper** and coat one slice at a time in **100 g/3¹/₂ oz flour**. Fry until crisp in a total of **8 tbsp hot olive oil** and allow to drain on a kitchen towel. Sweat **1 peeled and chopped onion** and **1 peeled and chopped garlic clove** in **1 tbsp hot olive oil** until translucent. Pour in **150 ml/¹/₄ pint each of vegetable stock, balsamic vinegar** and **dry white wine** and bring to the boil. Add **1 tsp crushed peppercorns**, **¹/₂ tsp sugar** and **1 tsp each of chopped rosemary, oregano, chopped parsley** and **lemon balm**. Pour the marinade over the courgettes and leave to stand for 15 minutes. Serve with herb curd cheese.

Preparation time: approx. 15 min., per portion: approx. 5 g P, 10 g F, 23 g C, 239 kcal

Courgette Fritters with Sheep's Cheese

Finely chop **250 g/9 oz cleaned and trimmed courgettes** in a food processor and mix with **200 g/7 oz crumbled sheep's cheese**. Stir in **2 eggs** and **1 bunch of mixed chopped herbs**. Mix together **50 g/1³/₄ oz flour, 1 tbsp cornflour** and **200 g/7 oz instant mashed potato powder** and work everything to a creamy mixture. Heat **2 tbsp olive oil** and in it fry, one at a time, 8 fritters until crisp. Serve with herb curd cheese or tzatziki.

Preparation time: approx. 25 min., per piece: approx. 15 g P, 18 g F, 18 g C, 152 kcal

Pickled Courgettes

For 6–7 250 ml/9 fl oz screw-top jars

Cut **1 kg/2¹/₄ lb courgettes** into roughly ½ cm/ 1/6 in slices, peel **200 g/ 7 oz onions** and cut into rings. Peel and thinly slice **4 garlic cloves.** Place **1 sprig of rosemary, thyme** and **oregano** in each screw-top jar and fill with all the ingredients. Bring to the boil **1 l/1³/₄ pints wine vinegar** with **500 ml/18 fl oz water, 1 tbsp salt, 100 g/3¹/₂ oz honey** and **1 tsp each of peppercorns, whole allspice, coriander** and **fennel seeds**. Pour over the courgettes while still hot. Seal the jars immediately and store in a dark place. Preserved in this way, courgettes will keep for about 10 months.

Preparation time: approx. 25 min., per jar: approx. 4 g P, 1 g F, 19 g C, 132 kcal

Mushroom Ragout in Herb Cream Sauce

Gently fry **2 peeled and chopped onions** in **2 tbsp hot butter** until translucent.

Add **500 g/1 lb 2 oz fresh woodland mushrooms** that have been cleaned, trimmed and finely cut, and gently cook everything together.

Pour in **8 tbsp white wine** and **400 ml/14 fl oz vegetable stock**, bring to the boil, stir in **6 tbsp cream** and season with **salt, pepper** and **cayenne pepper** according to taste.

Simmer for 5 minutes then fold in **8 tbsp chopped mixed herbs**. Arrange the mushroom ragout on plates. This dish tastes delicious served with gnocchi or bread dumplings.

Preparation time: approx. 20 min.,
per portion: approx. 10 g P,
11 g F, 38 g C, 305 kcal

Pan-Stirred Cabbage

Blanch separately for 2 minutes in boiling salted water **800 g/1¾ lb trimmed and shredded white cabbage** and **1 green pepper** with the seeds removed and cut into strips. Sauté **2 peeled and chopped onions, 1 peeled and chopped garlic clove** and **1 trimmed and chopped red chilli in 2 tbsp hot clarified butter**. Add the drained green pepper and shredded cabbage and gently simmer together. Stir in **2 tsp freshly-grated ginger, 2 tbsp tomato purée, 2 tbsp rice vinegar, 4 tbsp soy sauce** and **1 tsp brown sugar**. Pour in **250 ml/9 fl oz vegetable stock** and bring to the boil. Season with **salt** and **pepper**.

Preparation time: approx. 25 min., per portion: approx. 4 g P, 4 g F, 13 g C, 118 kcal

Aubergine and Coconut Pot

Bring **200 ml/7 fl oz coconut milk** and **1 tbsp yellow curry paste** to the boil in a saucepan. Add to the pan **100 g/3½ oz green aubergine** and **200 g/7 oz dark aubergine**, both trimmed and cut into chunks, **100 g/3½ oz sliced yellow courgette, 2 leeks** cut into rings and **2 finely-chopped red chillies** without the seeds and cook for about 2 minutes. Add **14 chopped borage leaves** and **3 tbsp** each of chopped **coriander** and **chopped parsley** and season according to taste with **salt, pepper** and **light soy sauce**. This dish is delicious served with basmati rice.

Preparation time: approx. 25 min.,
per portion: approx. 7 g P, 11 g F, 9 g C, 173 kcal

Tofu Strips with Mushrooms and Rice

200 g/7 oz tofu · salt · pepper · 2 tbsp lime juice · $^1/_2$ tsp curry powder · 2 tbsp soy sauce · 1 onion · 4 tbsp olive oil · 40 g/$1^1/_2$ oz oyster mushrooms · 1 tbsp flour · 100 g/ $3^1/_2$ oz crème fraîche · 3 tbsp white wine · nutmeg · cayenne pepper · 1 spring onion

Cut the tofu into strips, season with salt and pepper. Mix together the lime juice with curry powder and soy sauce and marinate for about 15 minutes. Peel and chop the onion and sweat until translucent in 2 tbsp oil. Clean and sort the oyster mushrooms, cut into small pieces, add to the onion and braise together. Sprinkle the flour over the mushrooms and onion and lightly brown.

Add the crème fraîche and wine and stir in. Season with nutmeg and cayenne pepper and simmer for 8 minutes. Drain the tofu strips and fry until crisp in a second pan with the remaining oil. Fold into the mushroom mixture and garnish with spring onion rings. Serve accompanied with long grain rice cooked according to the directions on the packet.

Preparation time: approx. 15 min., per portion: approx. 9 g P, 17 g F, 4 g C, 216 kcal

TIP

Tofu is made from soya milk. It is available in both a firm and a soft form. Use the firm type for this dish as it is easier to cut into strips. In addition to the mushrooms you can also add the vegetables of your choice.

Mixed Vegetables and Cream

Peel **400 g/14 oz white asparagus**, cut off the ends and chop the spears into chunks. Cut **200 g/7 oz green beans** into small pieces. Peel and slice **200 g/7 oz carrots**. Separate **350 g/12 oz cauliflower** into small florets. Blanch these vegetables and **100 g/3½ oz mangetout** separately in boiling salted water until al dente. Drain, retaining the cooking water, and rinse in iced water. Gently sauté **100 g/3½ oz of both finely cut button mushrooms** and **chanterelles** in **3 tbsp hot butter.** Remove from the pan. Melt **3 tbsp butter** in the pan and make a roux with **3 tbsp flour**, add **vegetable stock**, blend well by stirring and reduce until creamy. Season with **salt** and **pepper**. Add the vegetables and mushrooms to the sauce. Whisk together **2 egg yolks** and **100 ml/3½ fl oz cream**, stir into the sauce and season with **Worcester sauce** according to taste. Serve garnished with **2 tbsp freshly-chopped chervil**.

Preparation time: approx. 40 min., per portion: approx. 10 g P, 6 g F, 11 g C, 230 kcal

Vegetable Hotpot

Chop or slice **3 peeled onions, 250 g/9 oz scraped carrots, 2 yellow** and **2 green peppers, 200 g/7 oz trimmed courgettes** and **200 g/7 oz runner beans** and sauté in **3 tbsp rapeseed oil** while stirring.
Pour in **750 ml/1⅓ pints vegetable stock** and simmer with the lid on for 10 minutes. Add **400 g/14 oz diced tomatoes** and **1 bunch of chopped thyme** and bring back to the boil. Finally, stir in **150 g/5 oz sour cream** and serve.

Preparation time: approx. 20 min.,

per portion: approx. 7 g P, 7 g F, 15 g C, 162 kcal

Savoy Cabbage Hotpot with Nuts

1 onion • 2 carrots • 2 tbsp oil • 750 g/1 lb 10 oz Savoy cabbage • 200 g/7 oz red lentils • 750 ml/1¹⁄₃ pints vegetable stock • salt • pepper • 2 tbsp vinegar • 1 tbsp cornflour • 3 tbsp chopped walnuts

Peel the onion and carrots and slice and dice respectively. Heat the oil in a saucepan and sauté both vegetables together.
Rinse the Savoy cabbage, remove the hard stalk veins and cut the leaves into strips, add to the onion and carrots and briefly sauté.
Add the red lentils and pour in the vegetable stock, simmer everything for about 10 minutes.
Season according to taste with salt, pepper and vinegar. Mix the cornflour with a little water and use to bind the hotpot. Fold in the chopped walnuts and serve.

Preparation time: approx. 20 min., per portion: approx. 19 g P, 12 g F, 35 g C, 335 kcal

TIP
You can also use diced potato as a substitute for red lentils.

Red Cabbage with Nuts

Finely shred **700 g/1½ lb trimmed red cabbage**, removing the hard core. Gently sweat **3 tbsp spelt flour** in **2 tbsp hot butter**, pour in **500 ml/18 fl oz vegetable stock** and season with **salt, pepper** and **1 tsp lemon juice**. Heat the shredded red cabbage in the sauce for 5 minutes. Stir in **100 g/3½ oz crème fraîche** and sprinkle with **2 tbsp chopped roasted hazelnuts**.

Preparation time: approx. 20 min.,
per portion: approx. 4 g P, 12 g F,
10 g C, 175 kcal

Leek in Ricotta Sauce

Cut **800 g/1¾ lb cleaned and trimmed leeks** in 3 cm/1 in chunks and add to **200 ml/7 fl oz heated vegetable stock.** Stir together **400 g/ 14 oz ricotta** and **350 ml/12 fl oz milk** until smooth and add to the leeks. Season according to taste with **salt, pepper** and **nutmeg**. Stir in **1 tsp crushed red peppercorns** and cook everything together for about 8 minutes. Mix **1 tsp cornflour** with a little water and use to bind the ricotta sauce. Serve with sautéed potatoes.

Preparation time: approx. 15 min., per portion: approx. 18 g P, 12 g F, 13 g C, 244 kcal

Italian Vegetable Platter

250 g/9 oz courgettes · 1 red onion · 3 tbsp oil · 1 tbsp
lemon juice · salt · pepper · paprika powder · 1/2 bunch
Italian herbs · 250 g/9 oz baby carrots · 1 tsp vegetable
stock · 1/2 tsp sugar · 2 tbsp raspberry vinegar · 3 tbsp olive
oil · 2 sprigs of tarragon · 1 flatbread · 50 g/1 3/4 oz
herb butter

Trim and slice the courgettes, cut the onion into rings and gently
fry both in hot oil. Sprinkle with lemon juice and season with salt,
pepper and paprika. Add the chopped herbs.
Peel the carrots and cut lengthways into thin strips. Mix 6 tbsp
water with the vegetable stock, stir in the sugar and vinegar,
bring to the boil and use to blanch the carrot strips for about
5 minutes. Allow the carrot to cool in the liquid then drain in a
sieve. Mix with the olive oil. Add chopped tarragon and leave to
stand for 15 minutes.
Briefly warm the flatbread in the oven, break into pieces and
spread with the herb butter. Arrange on a platter together with
the vegetables and serve.

Preparation time: approx. 40 min., per portion: approx. 2 g P, 19 g F, 10 g C, 217 kcal

TIP

If you wish, you can also cut 1 aubergine into
thin slices, fry in hot oil and add to the vegetable
platter when cooled down.

Stir-Fried Courgettes and Tomatoes

Gently sauté **5 spring onions** cut into rings and **1 peeled and chopped garlic clove** in **2 tbsp hot olive oil**. Add **400 g/14 oz trimmed and sliced courgettes** and **300 g/ 11 oz tomatoes** cut into wedges with the stalk cores removed and gently cook everything for about 10 minutes while stirring. Season with **salt, pepper** and **1 tbsp each of both chopped thyme** and **chopped rosemary**. Serve with rice or pasta.

Preparation time: approx. 15 min., per portion: approx. 2 g P, 5 g F, 7 g C, 96 kcal

208

Spinach Cutlets

Rinse **1 kg/2¼ lb fresh spinach** and while still wet heat in a pan until it collapses, then drain and finely chop. Make a roux with **1 tbsp butter** and **1 tbsp flour**, stir in **125 ml/4 fl oz milk**, allow to thicken then season according to taste with **salt, pepper** and **nutmeg**. Sweat **1 chopped onion** and **1 chopped garlic clove** in **1 tbsp hot butter**. Combine the spinach, sauce, **1 egg**, and sweated onion into a mass and use to form cutlets of roughly 1 cm/⅓ in (add more flour if necessary). Beat **1 egg** and together with **50 g/1¾ oz flour** and **100 g/3½ oz breadcrumbs** place on a separate plate for each ingredient. Coat the spinach cutlets first in flour, then egg and finally breadcrumbs, and fry until golden brown in **3 tbsp clarified butter**.

Preparation time: approx. 30 min., per portion: approx. 14 g P, 8 g F, 26 g C, 235 kcal

Vegetable Cutlets in Choux Pastry

125 ml/4 fl oz vegetable stock · 1 tbsp olive oil · 1 tsp salt ·
1 tbsp wholemeal flour · 1 egg · 1 egg yolk · 500 g/
1 lb 2 oz mixed vegetables (e.g. carrots, courgettes, kohlrabi) · 1 tbsp freshly-chopped parsley · 1 tbsp chive rings ·
pepper · oat flakes

To make the choux pastry, boil the vegetable stock with oil and
salt. Add the flour and stir until the dough separates from the
bottom of the pan. Remove the pan from the heat, gradually stir
in the egg and egg yolk a little at a time. Allow the dough to
cool.
Clean and trim the vegetables, peeling and dicing when necessary. Cook al dente in boiling salted water, drain, press slightly to
remove excess water and leave to cool.
Mix the choux pastry with the vegetables, stir in the herbs and
season with salt and pepper. Stir in oat flakes if the mixture is
too moist. Form rounds of about 1.5 cm/$1/2$ in thickness from the
mixture, place on a baking tray lined with baking paper and bake
in the oven for about 20 minutes at 170°C/340ºF/Gas 3 (fan
oven 150°C/300ºF/Gas 2). Serve with hollandaise sauce.

Preparation time: approx. 30 min., per portion: approx. 3 g P, 4 g F, 4 g C, 69 kcal

TIP
These tasty vegetable cutlets can also be
prepared in advance and eaten cold at picnics
or as a snack at the office.

Avocado Mousse

Cut **3–4 ripe avocados** in half, remove the stones and scoop out the flesh. Crush with a fork and mix together with **the juice of 1–2 lemons, salt, pepper, 1 peeled and chopped garlic clove, 1 chopped red chilli** and **150 g/5 oz yoghurt**. Fold in **2 tbsp freshly-chopped parsley** and serve with freshly-baked bread.

Preparation time: approx. 15 min., per portion: approx. 5 g P, 41 g F, 8 g C, 425 kcal

Pickled Olives

For 4 250 ml/9 fl oz jars
Layer **1 kg/2¼ lb fresh green olives** in a large **1 l/1¾ pint jar.** Peel
and slice **1 onion** and **3 cloves of garlic**. Add to the olives together with
10 peppercorns. Mix **100 ml/3½ fl oz lemon vinegar** with **1 l/1¾ pints
olive oil, 1 tbsp herbal salt, 3 tbsp herbes de Provence** and **1 tsp sugar**
and stir together well. Pour the oil over the olives.

Pluck the leaves from **1 sprig of rosemary** and **1 sprig of
tarragon** and add to the olives. Leave the olives in the
sealed jar to stand in a warm place for 5 days. Shake several times then divide up into 4 jars. Cover with
brine. Olives pickled this way will keep for
about 18 months.

Preparation time: approx. 20 min., per jar: approx. 4 g P,
280 g F, 10 g C, 2550 kcal

Chanterelle Casserole with Vegetables

Sort and wash **500 g/1 lb 2 oz chanterelles**, and gently simmer in a little salted water for about 5 minutes. Cut **1 aubergine** into 1 cm/$^1/_3$ in slices, salt and leave to stand for 15 minutes.

Chop **1 onion** and **1 garlic clove** and gently sauté in **3 tbsp heated oil.** Then add one after another the rinsed aubergine slices, **1 leek** cut into rings, **3 diced tomatoes** and the chanterelles and cook for 3 minutes while stirring.

Pour in **200 ml/7 fl oz vegetable stock**, bring to the boil and remove from the heat. Allow to cool a little then stir in **2 beaten eggs.**

Add the mixture to a well-greased casserole dish and sprinkle with **150 g/ 5 oz Gouda cheese**. Bake in the oven for about 25 minutes at 180°C/355ºF/ Gas 4 (fan oven 160°C/320ºF/Gas 3).

Preparation time: approx. 20 min., per portion:

approx. 19 g P, 25 g F, 6 g C, 320 kcal

Lentil Fritters

For about 8 fritters

Cook **200 g/7 oz red lentils** for about 15 minutes in **500 ml/18 fl oz vegetable stock** with **1 bay leaf**. Gently fry **1 peeled and chopped onion** and **1 peeled and chopped garlic clove** in **1 tbsp hot olive oil**, braise together with **1 peeled and grated carrot**.

Fold into the lentils together with **60 g/2 oz wholemeal flour, 2 eggs, 3 tbsp oat flakes, 75 g/2½ oz crème fraîche** and **3 tbsp chopped herbs**. Form 8 small fritters and fry on both sides in **2 tbsp hot olive oil** for about 3 minutes.

Preparation time: approx. 15 min., per piece: approx. 10 g P, 8 g F, 20 g C, 188 kcal

Tabbouleh

200 g/7 oz bulgur · 1 bunch parsley · 4 sprigs of fresh mint ·
1/2 cucumber · 4 spring onions · 2 beef tomatoes · juice of
2 lemons · 4 tbsp olive oil · salt · pepper

Boil the bulgur in 500 ml/18 fl oz water for about 10 minutes,
remove from the heat and leave to swell for about 20 minutes.
Finely chop the parsley and mint. Peel and finely dice the
cucumber. Trim the spring onions and cut into rings. Remove the
stalk cores from the tomatoes and dice the flesh.
Loosen the bulgur with a fork and mix with the vegetables and
the herbs. Prepare a dressing with lemon juice, oil, salt and
pepper and pour over the salad. Leave to stand for at least
1 hour. Then stir well and serve.

Preparation time: approx. 30 min., per portion: approx. 6 g P, 6 g F, 41 g C, 241 kcal

TIP
Tabbouleh can also be prepared with wheat semolina
instead of bulgur. You can also vary the vegetables
used according to taste.

Stuffed Peppers

Cut off the tops of **4 red sweet peppers**, put the tops to one side to use as lids, and remove the seeds. Place in a casserole dish filled with **a little vegetable stock**, sprinkle with **2 tbsp olive oil** and bake in the oven for about 15 minutes at 150°C/300°F/Gas 2 (fan oven 130°C/265°F/Gas ½). Gently sauté **2 chopped** onions in **2 tbsp heat olive oil**. Add **1 chopped garlic clove, 1 diced courgette** and **250 g/9 oz oyster mushrooms** cut into strips and gently sear. Season with **salt, pepper, ½ tsp cayenne pepper** and **1 tsp chopped thyme**. Add **200 g/7 oz basmati rice** and cook for 1 minute. Add **400 g/14 oz tinned chopped tomatoes** with their juice and simmer everything for 15 minutes. Top up with vegetable stock if necessary until the rice is cooked and all the liquid soaked up. Fill the peppers with the rice mixture and bake for a further 30 minutes.

Preparation time: approx. 20 min., per portion: approx. 9 g P, 4 g F, 49 g C, 275 kcal

Swiss Chard Roulades

Mix **1 peeled and chopped onion** with **100 g/3½ oz instant mix for vegetarian burgers** and **200 ml/7 oz water.** Season with **salt, pepper and grated nutmeg**. Leave to swell for 10 minutes. Stir in **75 g/2½ oz grated Parmesan**. Remove the hard stems from **12 leaves of Swiss chard**, blanch for 2 minutes in boiling water, drain and spread with the burger mixture. Roll up and fasten with cocktail sticks. Fry on all sides in **2 tbsp hot oil,** stir in **200 ml/7 fl oz vegetable stock** and **3 tbsp tomato purée** and cook the roulades for about 15 minutes.

Preparation time: approx. 15 min., per portion: approx. 12 g P, 16 g F, 4 g C, 214 kcal

Tofu Cutlet with Spinach

400 g/14 oz Spinach · 1 onion · 3 tbsp vegetable oil · salt ·
pepper · nutmeg · 600 g/1 lb 5 oz smoked tofu · 100 g/
3¹/₂ oz breadcrumbs · grated peel of 1 untreated lemon ·
50 g/1³/₄ oz flour · 100 ml/3¹/₂ fl oz milk

Sort the spinach, trim, rinse, place in a saucepan while still wet and
allow to collapse while stirring. Remove from the pan and drain
well. Then chop.
Chop the onion and briefly sauté in 1 tbsp hot oil. Add the spinach
and sauté for about 5 minutes. Season with salt, pepper and nutmeg.
Drain the tofu and cut into 8 slices. Spread the spinach mixture over
4 slices then top with the remaining 4 slices. Mix the breadcrumbs
with the grated lemon peel. Dip each tofu cutlet first in flour, then
milk, then breadcrumbs. Heat 2 tbsp oil in a pan and fry the filled
cutlets on all sides for about 2 minutes until crisp. Serve accompanied by a tomato sauce.

Preparation time: approx. 30 min., per portion: approx. 30 g P, 17 g F, 31 g C, 410 kcal

TIP

Instead of spinach, you can also stuff the
tofu cutlets with grated courgettes or strips
of sweet peppers.

Tofu with Turnips

Cook **300 g/11 oz red lentils** in **500 ml boiling salted water** for about 10 minutes. Sauté **500 g/1 lb 2 oz each of peeled and quartered baby turnips** and **diced beetroot in 2 tbsp hot olive oil.** Pour in **300 ml/11 fl oz vegetable stock**, cover and simmer for 8 minutes. Finely dice **300 g drained tofu** and add to the root vegetables together with the drained lentils. Fold in **1 tbsp each of chopped chervil, chives** and **chopped parsley** and season with **salt** and **pepper** according to taste.

Preparation time: approx. 20 min., per portion: approx. 33 g P, 11 g F, 52 g C, 452 kcal

Pan-fried Peppers with Tofu

Prepare a marinade from **the juice and grated peel of 1 untreated lime, 1 chopped red chilli without seeds, 1/2 tsp coarsely-ground pepper** and **3 tbsp soy sauce** and use to marinate **400 g/14 oz diced tofu** for 15 minutes. Fry **1 diced red pepper, 1 diced yellow pepper** and **1 peeled and diced onion** in a wok with **1 tbsp hot peanut oil.** Remove from the wok. Coat the drained tofu cubes in **2 tbsp flour** and fry in **4 tbsp hot peanut oil** until crisp. Pour in the marinade and heat. Add the vegetables, heat through, season according to taste and serve.

Preparation time: approx. 20 min.,
per portion: approx. 17 g P,
12 g f, 6 g C, 215 kcal

Meat

Couscous Chicken Salad

Soak **200 g/7 oz couscous** in a mixture of **the juice of 2 lemons** and **250 ml/9 fl oz water** and allow to swell for 30 minutes. Then drain and mix with a marinade of **3 tbsp olive oil, 1 tsp balsamic vinegar, salt, pepper, sugar** according to taste and **1 generous pinch of cayenne pepper**. Mix with **1 skinned, de-seeded and diced large tomato**, **1/2 peeled and diced cucumber** and the diced flesh of **1 mango**. Thinly slice **400 g/14 oz cooked chicken breast** and serve with the salad.

Preparation time: approx. 25 min., per portion: approx. 25 g P, 25 g F, 27 g C, 443 kcal

Chicken Roulades with Pesto

Beat **4 chicken escalopes** until flat, spread with **150 g/5 oz pesto** from a jar and roll up. Fix the roulades with cocktail sticks or small wooden skewers. Heat **2 tbsp olive oil** in a pan and brown the chicken roulades well on all sides. Pour in **125 ml/4 fl oz vegetable stock** and cook the roulades for about 12 minutes.

Slice and serve with **salad**.

Preparation time: approx. 15 min., per portion: approx. 37 g P, 4 g F, 4 g C, 212 kcal

Saltimbocca

Beat flat **8 small escalopes of veal** and lay **1 slice air-dried ham** and **1 sage leaf** on each escalope. Fold the escalopes over and secure with a cocktail stick or small wooden skewer.

Fry the Saltimbocca on all sides in **2 tbsp heated oil** for about 4 minutes. Remove from the pan and keep warm. Bring the juices in the pan to the boil together with **200 ml/7 fl oz meat stock,** season according to taste with **1 tbsp lemon juice, 2 tbsp cream, salt** and **pepper** and serve with **pasta**.

Preparation time: approx. 20 min., per portion: approx. 33 g P, 9 g F, 3 g C, 257 kcal

Stuffed Escalope of Veal

Season **4 thin escalopes of veal** with **salt** and **pepper**, place **1 slice Parma ham** and **2 basil leaves** on each escalope, roll up and secure with cocktail sticks. Brown in **2 tbsp hot olive oil**, gently fry with **2 peeled and chopped shallots** for 2 minutes. Add **370 g/13 oz tinned chopped tomatoes** and simmer with the lid on for about 15 minutes. Then continue to simmer the sauce briefly after adding **5 tbsp sherry**. Season according to taste with **salt**, **pepper** and **sugar**. Serve with **ribbon pasta**.

Preparation time: approx. 15 min., per portion: approx. 33 g P, 6 g F, 37 g C, 355 kcal

Escalope of Turkey in Lemon

4 turkey escalopes · 10 tbsp lemon juice · 6 tbsp olive oil ·
1 onion · 1 green and 1 red pepper · salt · pepper

Trim the skin and sinews from the turkey escalopes and beat
flat between two layers of cling film. Mix the lemon juice with
3 tbsp olive oil and use to marinate the meat. Peel and chop the
onion, trim the peppers, remove the seeds and dice. Gently fry in
1 tbsp hot oil and braise for about 10 minutes. Season with salt
and pepper. Remove the meat from the marinade and allow to
drain. Heat up the remaining oil and fry the escalopes on both
sides for about 4 minutes.
Season and remove from the pan. Pour the marinade into the frying oil in the pan, bring to the boil and season according to taste.
Serve the turkey escalopes together with the lemon sauce and
the cooked peppers and accompanied by fresh baguette.

Preparation time: approx. 25 min., per portion: approx. 37 g P, 13 g F, 6 g C, 297 kcal

TIP
This dish is traditionally prepared with escalopes
of veal. It is worth trying it out sometime.

Fillet of Lamb with Green Asparagus

Cook only the top third of **500 g/1 lb 2 oz green asparagus** in boiling salted water for about 5 minutes. Drain and keep warm. Season **4 lamb fillets** with **salt** and **pepper** and fry on both sides for about 3 minutes in **3 tbsp hot butter**. Remove from the pan and keep warm.

Sweat **3 chopped garlic cloves** in the juices in the pan. Pour in **100 ml/ 3¹/₂ fl oz lamb stock** and reduce a little. Stir in **2 tbsp cold butter** to make the sauce creamy. Serve the sauce with the asparagus and lamb fillets accompanied by **hash browns**.

Preparation time: approx. 20 min., per portion: approx. 32 g P, 14 g F, 4 g C, 278 kcal

Lamb Cutlets with Orange Sauce

Rub **4 lamb cutlets** with a mixture of **2 crushed garlic cloves** and **5 tbsp olive oil** and leave to stand overnight. Heat up a pan and fry the marinated lamb cutlets on both sides for about 5 minutes. Remove and keep warm. Sweat **2 chopped shallots** in the juices from frying. Add **250 ml/9 fl oz meat stock** and **1 tbsp chopped thyme** and bring to the boil. Purée the sauce, stir in **3 tbsp orange marmalade** and simmer the sauce for about 5 minutes. Serve the lamb cutlets with the sauce.

Preparation time: approx. 20 min., per portion: approx. 44 g P, 14 g F, 12 g C, 367 kcal

Beef Salad

1 large lettuce • 2 carrots • 1 yellow pepper • 150 g/5 oz
cherry tomatoes • 200 g/7 oz beef steak • 1 tbsp oil • salt •
pepper • 2 tbsp freshly chopped basil • 75 g/2$^{1}/_{2}$ oz natural
yoghurt • 50 ml/1$^{3}/_{4}$ fl oz buttermilk • 3 tbsp freshly grated
Parmesan • 3 tbsp finely chopped onion • 3 tbsp mayonnaise •
2 tbsp freshly chopped parsley • 1 tbsp white wine vinegar •
1 crushed garlic clove

Spin the washed lettuce until dry and tear the leaves into small
pieces. Peel the carrots and cut into sticks, remove the seeds from
the trimmed pepper and dice. Cut the cherry tomatoes in half.
Arrange the vegetables on plates.
Cut the meat into strips. Fry in hot oil on all sides for about
3 minutes so that it is still pink inside. Remove the pan from the
heat, season the meat with salt and pepper and stir in the basil.
Place on top of the vegetables. Prepare a dressing with the
remaining ingredients and pour over the salad. Serve while
still warm.

Preparation time: approx. 30 min., per portion: approx. 16 g P, 9 g F, 11 g C, 194 kcal

TIP
You can replace the beef with poultry or strips of fillet of
lamb. If you wish, you can also add a chopped fresh red
chilli with the seeds removed to the salad dressing.

Chicken and Vegetable Casserole

Cut **4 chicken escalopes** into large chunks. Blanch **200 g/7 oz mangetout** in boiling water for about 2 minutes. Remove and drain.

Heat up **2 tbsp vegetable oil** and use to fry the pieces of meat lightly. Add **3 peeled and sliced carrots, 1 peeled and diced kohlrabi** and **200 g/7 oz cauliflower florets** to the meat and briefly sauté together.

Season with **salt, pepper** and **1 tbsp curry powder**.

Add **100 ml/3½ fl oz chicken stock** and **3 tbsp soy sauce** and simmer everything for about 5 minutes. Stir in the mangetout and **1 tbsp roasted sesame seeds** and season with **salt** and **pepper**. Serve with **rice**.

Preparation time: approx. 30 min., per portion:

approx. 42 g P, 7 g F, 12 g C, 287 kcal

Chicken with Pineapple and Ginger

Cut **400 g/14 oz chicken breast** into strips and coat with a mixture of **2 tsp cornflour, salt** and **pepper**. Heat **2 tbsp oil** in a wok and stir-fry the strips of meat for about 5 minutes. Stir in **250 g/9 oz drained tinned pineapple chunks**, season with **1 tsp ground ginger, 1 tsp curry powder** and **2 tbsp soy sauce,** cover with a lid and cook for a further 5 minutes. Serve with basmati rice.

Preparation time: approx. 20 min., per portion: approx. 28 g P, 3 g F, 61 g C, 400 kcal

Lamb's Lettuce with Melon and Chicken Breast

Sauté **4 chicken breasts** seasoned with **salt, pepper** and **mild paprika** in **2 tbsp hot vegetable oil** on both sides for about 5 minutes until they are completely cooked through. Remove from the pan, drain and allow to cool. Then cut into thin slices. Using a melon baller, scoop out the flesh of **¹/₂ small cantaloupe melon** and **¹/₂ small honeydew melon**, catching the juice. Make a dressing by mixing **a little melon juice** with **1 tbsp honey, 2 tbsp white wine vinegar, 2 tbsp vegetable oil, salt** and **pepper**. Mix in a bowl **400 g/14 oz lamb's lettuce, 4 spring onions** in thin rings, **2 tomatoes** cut into wedges and the melon balls and coat with the dressing. Arrange the chicken slices on top.

Preparation time: approx. 20 min., per portion: approx. 16 g P, 19 g F, 15 g C, 293 kcal

Turkey Rolls with Pesto

Beat flat **4 turkey escalopes** and spread with **150 g/5 oz red pesto** from a jar. Roll up the escalopes and fasten with a cocktail stick or small wooden skewer.

Heat **2 tbsp olive oil** and brown the turkey rolls well all over. Pour in **150 ml/5 fl oz vegetable stock** and cook for about 12 minutes.

Cut the turkey rolls into slices and serve garnished with **basil leaves** and accompanied by **hash browns** and **salad**.

Preparation time: approx. 10 min., per portion: approx. 37 g P, 4 g F, 4 g C, 212 kcal

Lamb Fritters with Sage Yoghurt

350 g/12 oz minced lamb • 1 onion • 4 tbsp breadcrumbs •
1 egg • 1 tbsp freshly chopped sage • salt • pepper • paprika
• 2 tbsp olive oil • 4 tbsp yoghurt • 1 tsp dried sage • 100 g/
3½ oz cucumber • ½ bunch parsley

Place the minced lamb in a bowl. Peel the onion, chop and add
to the bowl. Add the breadcrumbs and the egg and work to a
smooth mixture. Season with sage, salt, pepper and paprika.
Form 8 fritters from the mixture. Heat the olive oil in a pan and
fry the fritters on both sides for 8 minutes. Mix together the
yoghurt and the dried sage. Peel and dice the cucumber. Fold
into the yoghurt. Season with salt and pepper. Serve the lamb
fritters with the yoghurt and garnished with chopped parsley.

Preparation time: approx. 20 min., per portion: approx. 28 g P, 8 g F, 6 g C, 216 kcal

TIP
The yoghurt adds a refreshing note to these
fritters. Serve with sautéed potatoes or
toasted flatbread spread with herb butter.

Spinach Salad with Chicken and Parma Ham

Mix together **125 g/4¹/₂ oz sorted baby spinach, 75 g/2¹/₂ oz radicchio cut into strips** and **50 g/13/4 oz sliced mushrooms**. Cut **250 g/9 oz cooked chicken breast** and **50 g/1³/₄ oz Parma ham** into strips and fold into the mixture. Mix together **3 tbsp olive oil, 2 tbsp orange juice, 2 tbsp white balsamic vinegar, salt** and **pepper** and pour over the salad.

Preparation time: approx. 20 min., per portion: approx. 19 g P, 5 g F, 1 g C, 127 kcal

Chicken with Spinach and Chard Purée

Simmer **200 g/7 oz prepared fresh spinach** and **100 g/3 ½ oz finely cut Swiss chard** in **350 ml/12 fl oz water** for about 5 minutes. Drain, retaining 100 ml/3 1/2 fl oz of the cooking water. Purée the spinach and chard together with **1 tbsp peeled and grated ginger, 1 chopped green chilli** and **1 tsp ground coriander.** Roast **½ tsp cumin seeds** in **1 tbsp hot sunflower oil** until they burst. Fry **400 g/14 oz diced chicken breast** in the pan together with **1 more tbsp oil** for 3 minutes. Add the retained cooking water, cover and simmer for another 5 minutes. When the liquid has boiled away, stir in the spinach and chard purée and season according to taste with **salt** and **pepper**. Serve garnished with **1 tbsp roasted chopped almonds** and accompanied by freshly baked bread or rice.

Preparation time: approx. 20 min., per portion: approx. 26 g P, 7 g F, 2 g C, 186 kcal

Rump Steak with Mushrooms

Fry **4 rump steaks (each about 150 g/5 oz)** on both sides in **2 tbsp very hot oil.** Season with **salt** and **pepper**, remove from the pan and wrap in aluminium foil. Sauté **100 g/3½ oz sliced mushrooms** in the juices in the pan for 4 minutes. After 2 minutes add **3 peeled and chopped onions** and cook together.

Season with salt and pepper. Add **100 g/3½ oz cherry tomatoes** cut in half to the mushroom and onion mass and briefly cook together. Add the juices of the meat to the vegetables and arrange on plates together with the steaks. Sprinkle with **chopped parsley**. Serve with **baguette**.

Preparation time: approx. 20 min., per portion: approx. 47 g P, 9 g F, 11 g C, 322 kcal

Venison Steak with Figs

Fry **4 venison steaks** (each about 100 g/3½ oz) for about 3 minutes on both sides in **2 tbsp hot clarified butter**. Season with **salt** and **pepper** and keep warm. Deglaze the pan with **200 ml/7 fl oz white wine**, stir in **3 tbsp fig jam** and reduce slightly. Add **150 ml/5 fl oz cream** and season with salt and pepper according to taste. Top each steak with **½ a sliced fig** and serve with the sauce. Sautéed potatoes make a delicious accompaniment for this dish.

Preparation time: approx. 25 min., per portion: approx. 23 g P, 17 g F, 8 g C, 320 kcal

Lemon Chicken

6 chicken breast fillets · salt · pepper · 1 tbsp sweet paprika ·
50 g/1 3/4 oz flour · 8 tbsp butter · ½ bunch parsley ·
1 tsp dried tarragon · 5 tbsp lemon juice · 1 untreated lemon

Remove the skin and sinews from the chicken breasts and pat dry.
Beat the fillets flat and season with salt, pepper and paprika. Then
coat in flour and fry on both sides in 2 tbsp butter for about 5 minutes until cooked through. Remove from the pan and keep warm.
Melt the remaining butter in the pan. Finely chop the parsley and
sweat in the pan together with the tarragon. Stir in the lemon
juice and bring everything to the boil.
Lay the chicken fillets in the lemon butter. Wash the lemon under
hot water, pat dry and cut into slices. Use to garnish the chicken
fillets and serve with vegetable rice.

Preparation time: approx. 20 min., per portion: approx. 54 g P, 10 g F, 12 g C, 365 kcal

TIP
If you prefer a more Mediterranean variation,
sweat 1 tbsp each of freshly chopped thyme,
rosemary and oregano in the lemon butter.

Veal Roulades

Mix **125 g/5 oz sausage meat, 30 g/1 oz chopped chanterelles** from a jar with their liquid and **100 ml/3 1/2 fl oz meat stock** and season with **salt** and **pepper**. Beat **8 small escalopes of veal** until flat then season. Spread thinly with the sausage meat and roll up. Fasten with cocktail sticks or small wooden skewers.

Brown the veal roulades well all over in a pan with **3 tbsp hot clarified butter**, sauté together with **1 diced onion**. Sprinkle with **1 tbsp flour** and pour in **150 ml/5 fl oz veal stock**. Add **1 bouquet garni**, cover and simmer everything for about 35 minutes. Add more stock if necessary. Serve with **vegetable rice**.

Preparation time: approx. 20 min., per portion: approx. 37 g P, 20 g F, 6 g C, 405 kcal

Escalope of Veal in Marsala

Dust **4 escalopes of veal** with **2 tbsp seasoned flour (salt** and **pepper)** and sauté on both sides in **5 tbsp hot butter** for about 4 minutes. Remove from the pan and keep warm. Sauté **200 g/7 oz sorted and finely cut porcini mushrooms** in the butter used for frying, pour in **150 ml/5 fl oz Marsala** and simmer for 3 minutes. Season with **salt, pepper** and **1 tsp each of freshly chopped oregano** and **sage.**

Preparation time: approx. 20 min., per portion: approx. 28 g P, 9 g F, 3 g C, 236 kcal

Chinese Meat Salad

Fry **100 g/3¹/₂ oz tenderloin of pork** cut into strips in **2 tbsp hot oil** for about 4 minutes. Remove and place in a bowl. Cut **1 peeled baby turnip** and **1 peeled carrot** into strips, slice **2 celery stalks**, cut **100 g/3¹/₂ oz oyster mushrooms** into strips and **1 onion into rings,** and while stirring sauté everything together in the oil used for frying the pork for 3 minutes. Mix with the pork, **1 chopped garlic clove, 2 chopped spring onions** and **1 tsp grated ginger.** Mix together **3 tbsp soy sauce, 1¹/₂ tsp sesame oil, 1 tbsp sugar, 1 tsp rice vinegar, salt** and **pepper** and pour over the salad. Serve cooled sprinkled with **sesame seeds.**

Preparation time:
approx. 40 min.,
per portion:
approx. 9 g P, 8 g F,
9 g C, 145 kcal

250

Chinese Duck Breast Salad

Fry **4 duck breasts** on both sides in **3 tbsp hot oil** for 5–8 minutes, season with **salt** and **pepper**. Arrange on plates the cut-up leaves of **2 lettuces**, **2 shallots** sliced into rings, **4 chopped spring onions**, **1 celery stalk** in rings, **125 g/4¹/₂ oz cucumber** in strips, **125 g/4¹/₂ oz drained bean sprouts** and **200 g/7 oz drained and sliced tinned water chestnuts**. Top with the sliced duck breasts. Heat together **3 tbsp oyster sauce**, **1¹/₂ tbsp lime juice**, **2 chopped garlic cloves**, **1 chopped fresh red chilli** and **1 tsp honey** and pour over the salad.

Preparation time: approx. 30 min., per portion: approx. 30 g P, 30 g F, 15 g C, 448 kcal

Lamb with Honey Spinach

400 g/14 oz boned leg of lamb • salt • pepper • 1 tbsp soy sauce • 1 tbsp flour • 3 tbsp sesame oil • 1 onion • 2 garlic cloves • 450 g/1 lb spinach leaves • nutmeg • 1 tsp fruit vinegar • 1 tsp acacia honey • 40 g/1½ oz cold butter • 1 tsp cornflour • 125 ml/4 fl oz lamb stock • 1 tbsp freshly chopped peppermint leaves

Slice the lamb into thin strips, season with salt and pepper and sprinkle with soy sauce. Dust with flour. Heat up 2 tbsp oil in a pan or wok and stir-fry the lamb for about 2 minutes. Remove and keep warm. Peel and slice the onion and the garlic. Brown the onion slices in the pan/wok. Cut the spinach into strips, add to the pan and cook for 5 minutes until collapsed. Season with salt, pepper, nutmeg, vinegar and honey. Add the butter in flakes. Remove the spinach and keep warm. Heat the remaining oil in the pan/wok and roast the garlic. Add the cornflour and stir in the lamb stock. Stir in the chopped peppermint leaves. Heat the lamb in the sauce and serve with the spinach.

Preparation time: approx. 20 min., per portion: approx. 32 g P, 16 g F, 6 g C, 305 kcal

TIP

Instead of lamb, you can also prepare fillet of beef or chicken breast this way. Roast 1 tbsp sesame seeds and sprinkle them over the dish before serving.

Turkey Goulash

Sauté **1 peeled and chopped onion** in **2 tbsp clarified butter** until translucent. Add **450 g/1 lb ready-seasoned turkey goulash** and brown while stirring.

Add **500 g/1 lb 2 oz sauerkraut** and season with **salt, pepper, 1 tsp sugar** and **1 tsp sweet paprika**. Pour in **125 ml/4 fl oz vegetable stock** and cook together for 15 minutes. Fold in **4 tbsp sour cream** and season again according to taste. Serve with boiled potatoes.

Preparation time: approx. 15 min.,
per portion: approx. 29 g P, 10 g F, 5 g C, 234 kcal

Escalope of Chicken with Mushrooms

Sauté **500 g/1 lb 2 oz sliced mushrooms** in **2 tbsp hot butter** for about 10 minutes. Season with **salt** and **pepper**, add **a little lemon juice** according to taste and stir in **1/2 bunch of chopped parsley**. Keep warm.

Beat flat **4 chicken escalopes** and fry on both sides in **4 tbsp hot clarified butter** for about 6 minutes. Remove from the pan, dust with **curry powder** and keep warm.

Cut **16 cocktail tomatoes** in half and toss in the butter used for frying for about 5 minutes.

Serve the chicken escalopes with the mushrooms and tomatoes.

Preparation time: approx. 30 min., per portion: approx. 40 g P, 14 g F, 2 g C, 302 kcal

Stuffed Escalope of Turkey

8 thin turkey escalopes · salt · pepper · 8 thin slices of cooked ham · 16 sage leaves · 3 tbsp oil · 100 ml/3^1/$_2$ fl oz white wine · 125 ml/4 fl oz chicken stock · 100 g/3^1/$_2$ oz cold butter · 400 g/14 oz romanesco · nutmeg · 20 g/^{3}/$_4$ oz melted butter

Rinse the turkey escalopes, pat dry, beat lightly to flatten a little and season with salt and pepper. Top each escalope with 1 slice of ham and 2 sage leaves, roll up and fasten with cocktail sticks. Sauté on all sides in hot oil for 2 minutes and remove from the pan. Keep warm. Deglaze the pan with wine and stock, stir in the cold butter a piece at a time to bind the sauce. Divide the romanesco into florets and cook in boiling salted water for about 10 minutes. Drain and season with salt, pepper and ground nutmeg. Drizzle with the melted butter. Serve the turkey escalopes accompanied by the romanesco.

Preparation time: approx. 20 min., per portion: approx. 50 g P, 21 g F, 6 g C, 431 kcal

TIP
Romanesco is a variant form of cauliflower first grown in Rome. The florets have a green to violet colour. For this recipe you can also serve it sprinkled with breadcrumbs roasted in hot butter.

Chicken Salad with Vegetables

Fry **500 g/1 lb 2 oz strips of cleaned and trimmed chicken breast** on all sides in **2 tbsp hot oil** for about 3 minutes. Remove from the pan. Cut **3 peeled kohlrabies** into sticks and sauté for 5 minutes in **2 tbsp hot butter**. Blanch **150 g/5 oz cleaned and trimmed mangetout** in boiling water for about 3 minutes and cut into pieces when drained. Mix with the kohlrabi and coat with a sauce made from **5 tbsp sour cream, the juice of 1 lemon, salt, pepper, cayenne pepper** and **1 pinch nutmeg**. Stir together well, fold in the chicken strips and serve.

Preparation time: approx. 30 min.,
per portion: approx. 29 g P, 18 g F,
9 g C, 312 kcal

Chicken Salad with Mushrooms and Mandarin Oranges

Coat **400 g/14 oz chicken breast** in a mixture of **1 tsp salt, 1/2 tsp cayenne pepper, 1/2 tsp pepper** and **1/4 tsp chopped thyme**. Fry on both sides in **2 tbsp hot oil** for about 7–8 minutes. Allow to drain. Mix together **275 g/10 oz shredded iceberg lettuce, 50 g/1³/₄ oz chopped pecan nuts** and **300 g/11 oz drained tinned mandarin oranges**. Mix **2 tbsp orange juice** with **2 tbsp rice wine vinegar, 4 tbsp olive oil, sugar** according to taste, **salt** and **pepper** and pour over the salad. Top with the strips of chicken and serve.

Preparation time: approx. 30 min., per portion:

approx. 28 g P, 15 g F, 19 g C, 325 kcal

Medallions of Venison
with Pumpkin Vegetables

300 g/11 oz patisson pumpkin · salt · pepper · 1/2 tsp
nutmeg · 4 medallions of venison (each about 120 g/4 oz) ·
1 onion · 2 tbsp oil · 150 ml/5 fl oz game stock · 150 ml/
5 fl oz dry red wine · 100 g/3 1/2 oz dried apricots · 2 tbsp
cranberry jelly · 2 tbsp cornflour · 2 tbsp brandy · 2 tbsp
freshly chopped parsley

Peel the pumpkin, cut into chunks and cook in boiling salted water
for about 15 minutes. Season with salt, pepper and nutmeg.
Remove the skin and sinews from the meat and season with salt
and pepper. Peel and finely chop the onion. Heat the oil in a
roasting pan and sweat the onion until translucent.
Add the medallions and seal on both sides for about 2 minutes.
Pour in the game stock and red wine and turn down the heat.
Add the chopped dried apricots and dissolve the cranberry jelly in
the sauce while stirring. Simmer everything for about 10 minutes.
Remove the medallions from the pan and keep warm. Mix the
cornflour with the brandy until smooth and use to bind the sauce.
Season according to taste. Arrange the medallions on plates
together with the pumpkin and sauce and serve sprinkled with
parsley.

Preparation time: approx. 30 min., per portion: approx. 32 g P, 9 g F, 24 g C, 350 kcal

TIP
You can also use fillet of beef instead of venison. This
dish is also delicious with braised red cabbage or Savoy
cabbage instead of pumpkin. Serve with spaetzle, a
traditional German pasta from the Swabian region.

Chicken Salad with Asparagus and Mushrooms

Finely dice the meat of **a ½ cooked chicken**. Mix with **100 g/3½ oz drained asparagus tips** from a jar, **125 g/4½ oz sliced mushrooms**, **1 diced pineapple ring** and **1 peeled, cored and diced apple**. Mix together **4 tbsp salad cream**, **75 g/2½ oz yoghurt**, **salt**, **pepper**, **1 tsp curry powder**, **1 pinch sugar** and **1 tbsp fruit vinegar** and pour over the salad.

Preparation time: approx. 20 min., per portion: approx. 11 g P, 4 g F, 12 g C, 130 kcal

Game Salad with Mushrooms

Leave **160 g/5¹/2 oz ready-to-cook filleted saddle of hare** to stand in
200 ml/7 fl oz boiling game stock for about 10 minutes. Remove from the
stock and allow to cool.

Sauté **1 chopped onion** in **1 tbsp hot oil**. Cook together with **150 g/5 oz
sliced mushrooms** and **75 g/2¹/2 oz cleaned and trimmed chanterelles**
for 3 minutes, season with **salt** and **pepper**. Pour in **1 tbsp vinegar** and
5 tbsp game stock and leave to cool down.

Slice the hare fillets into strips and mix with the mushrooms. Arrange on a
bed of **100 g/3¹/2 oz cleaned and sorted lamb's lettuce**. Mix together
60 g/2 oz sour cream, 2 tbsp raspberry vinegar and **¹/2 tsp mustard** and
pour over the salad. Serve sprinkled with **¹/2 bunch chives** cut into rings.

Preparation time: approx. 40 min., per portion: approx. 15 g P, 7 g F, 3 g C, 138 kcal

Chicken with Cashew Nuts and Lemongrass

400 g/14 oz filleted chicken breast • 2 stalks lemongrass •
1/2 bunch spring onions • salt • pepper • 2 red chillies •
100 g/3¹/₂ oz cashew nuts • 3 tbsp vegetable oil • 1 tsp sugar
• 3 tbsp soy sauce • 2 tbsp freshly chopped coriander

Remove the skin and sinews from the chicken breast and cut into
strips. Peel and finely chop the lemongrass, clean, trim and cut
the spring onions into rings. Mix the chicken strips with the lemongrass, spring onions, salt and pepper and leave to stand for
20 minutes. Clean and trim the chillies, remove the seeds and
finely chop. Chop the cashew nuts in a food processor and roast in
a pan without fat. Remove and put to one side. Heat oil in a wok
and stir-fry the chicken strips for 4 minutes. Add the chilli and fry
together for 3 minutes. Season according to taste with sugar and
soy sauce. Fold in the cashew nuts. Serve sprinkled with the freshly chopped coriander.

Preparation time: approx. 15 min., per portion: approx. 28 g P, 15 g F, 10 g C, 290 kcal

TIP
If you find this dish too hot, leave out the chillies and
season sparingly with ground chilli instead. You can also
use unsalted peanuts instead of the cashew nuts.

Venison Steak with Peaches

Lightly pound **4 venison steaks** with the skin and sinews removed, place in a bowl, rub with a marinade made from **6 tbsp oil, 1/2 tsp pepper, 1 tbsp chopped marjoram** and **salt** and leave to stand for about 10 minutes. Peel **8 peaches**, cut in half, remove the stones and cut the fruit into wedges. Fry the steaks on both sides for about 4 minutes in a hot pan, lightly pressing them down. Keep warm. Sauté the peach wedges for 2 minutes in the juices from frying, then place on top of the steaks. Deglaze the pan with **125 ml/ 4 fl oz peach juice** and **125 ml/4 fl oz water** and stir in **1 sachet rich gravy** mix. Bring to the boil and season with **1 tbsp brandy**. Serve with the steaks accompanied by spaetzle, a traditional German pasta from the Swabian region.

Preparation time: approx. 20 min.,
per portion: approx. 34 g P, 10 g F, 34 g C, 377 kcal

Saddle of Venison

Rub **1.5 kg/approx. 3¹/₄ lb saddle of venison** with **salt, pepper** and **dried coriander**. Line an oven drip pan with **50 g/1³/₄ oz thinly cut bacon rashers**, lay the venison on top and cover with another **50 g/1³/₄ oz thinly cut bacon rashers**.

Add **2 quartered onions** and **5 crushed juniper berries** and roast the venison in the oven for 45–60 minutes at 200°C/390ºF/Gas 6 (fan oven 180°C/355ºF/Gas 4). Occasionally pour on a little hot water and baste with the juices from roasting. After roasting, separate the meat from the bone, cut into slices, replace on the bone and keep warm. Add water to the roasting juices to give 400 ml/14 fl oz. Mix together **100 g/3¹/₂ oz sour cream** and **2 tbsp flour** and use to bind the juices. Season according to taste and serve with the meat.

Preparation time: approx. 25 min., per portion: approx. 42 g P, 9 g F, 4 g C, 268 kcal

Ribbon Noodles with Beef Strips and Broccoli

While stirring, sauté **1 peeled and chopped onion** and **1 peeled and chopped garlic clove** together with **2 cm/³/₄ in peeled and finely chopped ginger** in **2 tbsp hot oil**. Add **400 g/14 oz broccoli florets**, season with **a little salt,** and while stirring gently cook everything for 4 minutes. Add **250 g/9 oz beef** sliced into thin strips. Add **150 g/5 oz finely cut shiitake mushrooms, 1 tbsp soy sauce** and **5 tbsp vegetable stock** and gently cook for 5 minutes. Season according to taste with **salt, pepper** and **a little sugar**. Serve with **400 g/14 oz ribbon pasta**.

Preparation time: approx. 20 min., per portion: approx. 29 g P, 11 g F, 77 g C, 530 kcal

Beef from the Wok with Grapes

Brown **500 g/1 lb 2 oz fillet of beef** with **2 cm/³/₄ in peeled and grated ginger** in a wok containing **1 tbsp hot oil**. Remove from the wok. Heat up **1 tbsp oil** in the wok and fry **1 diced red and 1 diced green pepper** and **100 g/3¹/₂ oz sliced mushrooms** for 3 minutes. Add **6 plums**, cut in half and with the stones removed, and fry for another 2 minutes. Mix together **250 ml/9 fl oz prune juice, 2 tbsp lemon juice, 2 tbsp soy sauce** and **1 tbsp cornflour** and add to the wok. Season with **¹/₄ tsp ground cinnamon, ¹/₄ tsp mustard powder** and **1 tbsp grated untreated orange peel** and bring to the boil. Cook the sauce until smooth and creamy. Add the beef and ginger and serve accompanied by rice.

Preparation time: approx. 20 min.,
per portion: approx. 29 g P, 8 g F, 23 g C,
292 kcal

Grilled Escalope of Turkey with Mango Chutney

4 escalopes of turkey (150 g/5 oz each) • 3 tbsp oil •
1 tbsp brandy • salt • pepper • $^1/_2$ tsp paprika • 4 tomatoes •
1 tbsp butter • 4 tbsp mango chutney

Wash the escalopes, pat dry and place in a bowl. Mix the oil together with the brandy, salt, pepper and paprika and pour over the escalopes. Leave to marinate for about 10 minutes. Wash the tomatoes, cut out the stalk cores and cut crosses into the tops. Place a little butter in the cuts and squeeze apart. Drain the marinated escalopes and grill on both sides for about 5 minutes over a preheated grill. Also grill the tomatoes. Serve each escalope garnished with 1 tbsp mango chutney and accompanied by a tomato. It can be served with either rice or fresh baguette.

Preparation time: approx. 15 min., per portion: approx. 37 g P, 7 g F, 8 g C, 262 kcal

TIP

Instead of mango chutney, you can also serve the escalopes with either 1 tbsp herb crème-fraîche or poached kumquats.

Beef Salad with Glass Noodles

Fry **200 g/7 oz beef strips** in **2 tbsp hot oil** for 1 minute.

Add **1 yellow pepper** with the seeds removed and cut into strips, **1 leek** cut into rings, **1 finely chopped red chilli** and fry everything for a further 2 minutes. Stir in **75 g/2¹/₂ oz glass noodles** that have been softened in warm water then squeezed out and briefly fry together. Put everything in a bowl to cool down. Mix together **4 tbsp rice wine vinegar, 4 tbsp oyster sauce, salt, pepper** and **sugar** according to taste. Mix with the salad and serve.

Preparation time: approx. 20 min., per portion: approx. 13 g P, 8 g F, 12 g C, 168 kcal

Turkey and Vegetable Salad

Mix **150 g/5 oz cooked ham** in strips with **150 g/5 oz cooked turkey breast**, **100 g/3$\frac{1}{2}$ oz trimmed celery**, **1 peeled carrot** and **40 g/1$\frac{1}{2}$ oz Emmental cheese** in strips. Fold in **2 chopped shallots**. Mix **2 tbsp white wine vinegar** together with **2 tsp mustard**, **$\frac{1}{4}$ tsp sweet paprika**, **salt** and **pepper** and pour over the salad. Leave to stand for 30 minutes. Serve garnished with **2 tbsp freshly cut chive rings**.

Preparation time: approx. 15 min., per portion: approx. 22 g P, 11 g F, 3 g C, 202 kcal

Turkey Strips with Vegetables

Fry **4 escalopes of turkey** (about 500 g/1 lb 2 oz) cut into strips on all sides in **2 tbsp hot clarified butter** and season with **salt** and **pepper**. Sprinkle with **1 tbsp flour** and sweat. Add **1 bunch of diced vegetables** for stock and briefly sauté together. Pour in **200 ml/7 fl oz vegetable stock** and **200 ml/ 7 fl oz cream** and simmer for about 10 minutes. Season according to taste with **salt, pepper and 3–4 tbsp Noilly Prat**. Serve sprinkled with **1/2 bunch of chopped chives**. Pasta goes well with this dish.

Preparation time: approx. 25 min., per portion: approx. 38 g P, 19 g F, 38 g C, 490 kcal

Fillet of Rabbit with Chanterelles

Rub **2 rabbit fillets (about 800 g/1 lb 12 oz)** with **salt** and **pepper** and brown on all sides in **20 g/³/₄ oz melted butter**. Cover and bake in the oven for 15 minutes at 120°C/250°F/Gas 1/2 (fan oven 100°C/210°F/ Gas 0). Clean, trim and cut up **500 g/1 lb 2 oz chanterelles** and **mushrooms**. Sauté in **2 tbsp hot oil** and **20 g/³/₄ oz butter** for about 5 minutes. Gently fry together with **2 spring onions** in rings and **1 tbsp freshly chopped thyme**. Season with **salt** and **pepper**.
Slice the rabbit fillets and arrange on top of the mushrooms. Serve with fresh **baguette**.

Preparation time: approx. 20 min., per portion: approx. 21 g P, 16 g F, 32 g C, 360 kcal

Mixed Salad with Roast Beef

Mix together **200 g/7 oz cleaned and trimmed lettuce, 1 green** and **1 red pepper** with the seeds removed and cut into strips, **4 diced tomatoes** and **200 g/7 oz sliced courgettes**. Add **100 g/3½ oz fried roast beef** in strips and **150 g/5 oz diced sheep's cheese**. Sprinkle with **1 tbsp each of wheat germ oil** and **balsamic vinegar**. Mix together **the juices of ½ lemon** and **1 orange, 150 g/5 oz sour cream, a chopped shallot, 50 g/1¾ oz chopped gherkins, salt, pepper, cayenne pepper** and **sugar** according to taste and mix with the salad. Serve sprinkled with **2 tbsp freshly chopped chervil**.

Preparation time: approx. 30 min., per portion: approx. 17 g P, 14 g F, 12 g C, 245 kcal

Beef Stroganoff

Cut **600 g/1 lb 5 oz fillet of beef** across the fibre into thin strips and briefly fry in small portions in **3 tbsp hot oil** and **10 g/⅓ oz butter**. Season with **salt** and **pepper**. Remove from the pan and keep warm. Sweat **300 g/ 11 oz small sliced mushrooms** and **2 chopped onions** in the oil used for frying the meat. Add **3 finely cut gherkins**, pour in **200 ml/7 fl oz beef stock**, stir in **2 tsp hot mustard** and allow the sauce to reduce and thicken slightly. Mix together **4 tbsp crème fraîche** and **1 tbsp cornflour** and use to bind the boiling sauce. Add the meat and heat through. Season according to taste and serve with **rice**.

Preparation time: approx. 20 min.,
per portion: approx. 8 g P, 12 g F, 6 g C, 174 kcal

Chicken with Oyster Mushrooms and Mangetout

500 g/1 lb 2 oz chicken breast · 400 g/14 oz mangetout ·
400 g/14 oz carrots · 150 g/5 oz oyster mushrooms · 4 tbsp
oil · 200 ml/7 fl oz vegetable stock · 2 tbsp soy sauce · salt ·
pepper

Pat the chicken breast dry and cut into strips. Clean and sort the
mangetout, remove any stringy fibres. Scrub the carrots and cut
into slices. Sort and trim the mushrooms, rub with a damp cloth
and cut up into small pieces. Brown the chicken strips on all sides
in hot oil. Add the mangetout, carrots and mushrooms and sauté
together for 2 minutes. Pour in the stock and simmer everything
for about 8 minutes. Season with soy sauce, salt and pepper. Rice
goes well with this dish.

Preparation time: approx. 20 min., per portion: approx. 36 g P, 7 g F, 13 g C, 270 kcal

TIP

Also try this recipe with 500 g/1 lb 2 oz beef cut into
strips. Before frying, marinate it for 5 minutes in 3 tbsp
soy sauce and season with 1 tsp five-spice powder.

Turkey Steak with Onion Vegetables

Season **4 turkey steaks** with **salt, pepper** and **1 pinch each of cayenne pepper** and **curry powder** and fry on both sides for 4 minutes in **2 tbsp hot oil**.

Remove from the pan and keep warm. Gently fry **400 g/14 oz peeled and thinly sliced onions** in the oil in the pan, add **2 tbsp tomato purée** and **8 tbsp white wine** and simmer for 4 minutes. Season with **1 tsp dried oregano** and **salt, pepper** and **curry powder** according to taste.

Stir in **2 diced tomatoes**, sprinkle with **2 tbsp freshly chopped chervil** and serve together with the turkey steaks.

Preparation time: approx. 20 min., per portion: approx. 38 g P, 4 g F, 7 g C, 231 kcal

Mixed Salad with Fillet of Hare

Mix together **150 g/5 oz trimmed and cooked green beans, 200 g/7 oz cleaned, sorted and cut-up mixed lettuce leaves, 100 g/3½ oz sliced mushrooms** and **1 peeled, cored and diced pear** and sprinkle with **the juice of ½ a lemon**. Fry **200 g/7 oz fillet of hare** in **2 tbsp hot oil** for about 5 minutes. Wrap in aluminium foil. Stir **2 tbsp red wine, 1 tsp mustard, 3 tbsp balsamic vinegar** and **5 tbsp oil** into the juices in the pan and mix together. Arrange the salad ingredients on plates and drizzle with the dressing. Cut the fillet of hare into slices and arrange on top of the salad.

Preparation time: approx. 30 min., per portion: approx. 13 g P, 4 g F, 7 g C, 121 kcal

Salad Surprise

Mix **200 g/7 oz cleaned and sorted cos lettuce** leaves cut into small pieces and **100 g/3½ oz cleaned, sorted and cut-up radicchio leaves** together with **1 chopped shallot, 1 peeled and diced carrot, 1 diced red pepper** and **100 g/3½ oz sliced mushrooms**. Fold in **100 g/3½ oz diced cooked turkey** and **100 g/3½ oz tinned tuna in oil** loosened into flakes. Add **100 g/3½ oz diced fontina cheese, 4 diced tomatoes** and **100 g/ 3½ oz sliced stoned olives**. Mix together **4 tbsp balsamic vinegar** with **6 tbsp olive oil, salt** and **pepper** and pour over the salad.

Preparation time: approx. 30 min.,
per portion: approx. 16 g P, 28 g F, 8 g C, 348 kcal

Veal in Tuna Sauce

For 8 portions

Make several incisions in the topside of **1 kg/2¼ lb veal** and stuff with **1 garlic clove** cut into sticks and **3 anchovy fillets**. Bring the meat to the boil in a saucepan with some water and simmer for 1 hour. Remove and simmer in another pan together with **2 peeled and diced carrots, 50 g/ 1¾ oz peeled and diced celeriac, 1 onion cut in half, 1⅛ l/2 pints veal stock, 5 peppercorns** and **2 bay leaves** for about 1½ hours. Remove and put aside until cold. Blend to a purée **150 ml/5 fl oz oil, 1 egg yolk, the flaked tuna from a tin, 3 anchovy fillets, 2 tbsp lemon juice** and **2 tbsp capers**. Season with **salt** and **pepper**. Thinly slice the meat and arrange with the sauce.

Preparation time: approx. 210 min., per portion: approx. 33 g P, 18 g F, 3 g C, 304 kcal

Fish

Norway Haddock with Vegetables

Cut **250 g/9 oz peeled carrots,
2 courgettes** and **2 yellow peppers** into thin strips. Lightly fry **1 peeled and chopped onion** and **30 g peeled and chopped ginger** in **2 tbsp hot sesame oil**, add **1 pinch cumin** and sauté together with all the vegetables for 5 minutes until al dente. Cook **½ bunch spring onions** cut into rings and **200 g/7 oz Norway Haddock** cut into chunks with the vegetable for 3 minutes. Pour in **250 ml/9 fl oz vegetable stock** and **2 tbsp soy sauce** and season according to taste with **salt** and **pepper**. Serve sprinkled with **2 tbsp freshly chopped coriander**.

Preparation time: approx. 20 min., per portion: approx. 13 g P, 7 g F, 8 g C, 154 kcal

Grilled Scampi on Salad

Marinate **300 g/11 oz peeled scampi** for about 3 hours in a mixture of **8 tbsp olive oil, 1 crushed garlic clove, salt** and **1 pinch chilli powder**. Mix **250 g/9 oz drained tinned sweet corn** with **1 diced red pepper, 1 diced green pepper** and **1 iceberg lettuce** cut into strips. Grill the prawns on an oiled baking tray in the oven on each side for 2 minutes. Blend **100 g/3½ oz stoned black olives** to a purée together with **1 crushed garlic clove, 3 tbsp lemon juice, salt** and **pepper**, fold in **2 tbsp chopped parsley**. Pour over the salad. Serve topped with the scampi.

Preparation time: approx. 40 min., per portion: approx. 18 g P, 21 g F, 12 g C, 310 kcal

Salmon Steak with Fennel

Sprinkle **4 salmon steaks (150 g/5 oz each)** with the juice of **1 lemon**, season with **salt** and **pepper** and fry on both sides for about 3 minutes in **2 tbsp hot oil** with **2 tsp hot butter**. Add to the fish **2 trimmed fennel bulbs** cut into strips and **4 peeled carrots** cut into strips and briefly sauté together. Pour in **150 ml/5 fl oz vegetable stock**, cover and cook everything for about 15 minutes. Season with **salt** and **pepper**. Arrange the salmon on the vegetables, top each steak with a **knob of herb butter** and serve sprinkled with **chopped dill** and accompanied by new potatoes.

Preparation time: approx. 15 min.,
per portion:
approx. 31 g P,
15 g F, 8 g C,
380 kcal

Pike with Rocket and Capers

Season **4 pike fillets** with **salt** and **pepper**, sprinkle with **2 tbsp lemon juice**. Heat up **75 g/2½ oz butter** and use to sweat **1 peeled and chopped garlic clove, 1 tbsp chopped capers** and **1 bunch of chopped rocket leaves** until the rocket collapses. Add **2 tbsp fish stock** and **1 tbsp lemon juice**, season with **salt, pepper** and **cayenne pepper**. Place the pike fillets on top and cook for about 3 minutes on both sides. Serve with the rocket and caper butter and accompanied by basmati rice.

Preparation time: approx. 30 min., per portion: approx. 31 g P, 17 g F, 21 g C, 372 kcal

Fillet of Sole with Mushrooms

800 g/1 lb 12 oz sole fillets · 1 tbsp lemon juice · salt ·
pepper · 500 g/1 lb 2 oz king oyster mushrooms · 1 onion ·
2 tbsp butter · 100 ml/3½ fl oz white wine · 4 tbsp crème
fraîche · 1 pinch cayenne pepper · ½ bunch flat-leaf parsley

Sprinkle the fillets of sole with lemon juice, season with salt and
pepper. Separate into 4 pieces. Clean and trim the oyster mushrooms and cut into small pieces. Season. Peel and chop the
onion. Heat the butter and sweat the onion until translucent.
Add the mushrooms and sauté together for 5 minutes. Stir in the
wine and crème fraîche and season with salt and cayenne pepper. Roll up the fish fillets and place on top of the mushrooms.
Cover and cook for about 8 minutes over a low heat. Serve
sprinkled with chopped parsley.

Preparation time: approx. 20 min., per portion: approx. 39 g P, 6 g F, 3 g C, 245 kcal

TIP

How to tell if fish is fresh: the meat should be moist and
clear, firm and white, and the cut surface smooth. Fish and
fish fillets should be kept on ice in the shop. Melting water
should be able to flow away. The fish should only smell of
the sea and seaweed, and not fishy.

Fish with Glazed Carrots

Peel **1 organic orange** with a zester. Fillet the orange catching the juice and use to drizzle over **400 g/14 oz filleted haddock**. Cover with the zest and a little **black pepper**. Leave to stand for 10 minutes. While stirring, caramelise in a pan **1 tsp butter** with **1 tsp sugar**, add and glaze **400 g/14 oz grated carrot**, cover and cook for about 2 minutes. Salt the carrots and add **4 tbsp vegetable stock.** Season the filleted fish and add to the carrots together with the marinade. Cover and simmer for about 10 minutes. Add the fillets of orange and heat through. Serve sprinkled with **chopped chives** and accompanied by boiled potatoes.

Preparation time:
approx. 15 min.,
per portion: approx. 20 g P,
5 g F, 11 g C, 175 kcal

292

Fillet of Sole on Onions

Salt and pepper **600 g/1 lb 5 oz sole fillets** and brush with **5 tbsp melted butter.**

Cut **1½ bunches of spring onions** into 3 cm/1 in pieces and briefly stir-fry in **2 tbsp hot oil**. Pour in **100 ml/3 1/2 fl oz white wine** and **100 ml/3½ fl oz vegetable stock** and allow to thicken slightly. Place the fish fillets on top of the onions, cover and braise for about 5 minutes. Remove the fillets and season the onions with **50 g/1¾ oz sour cream, salt** and **pepper** according to taste. Fold in **1 tbsp chopped chervil**.
Arrange the fish on top of the onions.
Serve with rice.

Preparation time: approx. 20 min.,
per portion: approx. 31 g P, 11 g F,
49 g C, 445 kcal

Cos Lettuce with Shrimps

Cut **2 heads of cos lettuce** into strips and mix together with **2 peeled and sliced kiwis,** **1/2 peeled, de-seeded and diced cantaloupe melon,** and **150 g/5 oz cooked shrimps**. Mix together **1 tbsp raspberry vinegar,** **2 tbsp soy sauce** and **1/2 peeled, de-seeded and puréed cantaloupe melon**, season according to taste with **salt** and **pepper** and fold in **1 bunch of chopped coriander**. Pour the dressing over the salad and serve garnished with **slices of kiwi.**

Preparation time: approx. 20 min., per portion: approx. 8 g P, 4 g F, 6 g C, 91 kcal

Prawn Cocktail with Asparagus

Cook **500 g/1 lb 2 oz each of trimmed white and green asparagus** in boiling water seasoned with **1 pinch of sugar, salt** and **a little butter** for about 10 (white) and 8 (green) minutes respectively. Remove, drain, allow to cool and cut into 5 cm/2 in pieces. Cook **300 g/11 oz unpeeled king prawns** in the asparagus water for 2 minutes, drain, allow to cool then peel. Remove the veins. Mix together with the asparagus and **1 peeled, deseeded and diced papaya**. Prepare a dressing with **the juice of 1 orange, 150 g/5 oz sour cream, 2 tbsp lemon juice, 2 tbsp oil, 4 tbsp tomato ketchup, 2 tbsp brandy, salt, pepper** and **1 bunch of chopped dill** and pour over the salad.

Preparation time: approx. 40 min., per portion: approx. 22 g P, 10 g F, 11 g C, 228 kcal

Grilled Trout with Herbs

4 ready-to-cook trout · 2 tbsp lemon juice · salt · pepper ·
100 ml/3¹/₂ fl oz olive oil · 1 bunch mixed herbs · 2 lemons

Rinse the trout well both inside and outside and pat dry.
Prepare a marinade with lemon juice, salt, pepper and olive oil
and use to brush the trout. Finely chop the rinsed herbs and place
inside the trouts' stomach. Lay the fish on the grill and grill on
both sides for about 6–8 minutes. Brush repeatedly with the
marinade. Serve garnished with lemon wedges and with a
mixed salad.

Preparation time: approx. 20 min., per portion: approx. 31 g P, 10 g F, 6 g C, 255 kcal

TIP

Other fish, dorado for example, are also suitable for grilling
until crisp. Filleted fish is best grilled when wrapped in
aluminium foil so it can cook in its own juices.

Fillet of Fish à l'Orange

Season **8 haddock fillets** with **salt** and **pepper**, sprinkle with **2 tbsp lemon juice** and cover with the **juice of 2 oranges**. Leave to stand for 10 minutes. Place the fish fillets in a greased casserole dish and sprinkle with **1 tsp dried oregano**. Peel **2 oranges**, cut into wedges and place on top of the fish. Mix together **250 ml/9 fl oz cream**, **2 tsp cornflour** and **2 tsp finely grated orange peel**, pour over the fish and bake in the oven for about 15 minutes at 200°C/390ºF/Gas 6(fan oven 180°C/355ºF/Gas 4). Serve with **saffron rice**.

Preparation time: approx. 10 min., per portion: approx. 30 g P, 20 g F, 19 g C, 382 kcal

Fish Mousse with Endives

Blend to a purée **250 g/9 oz smoked fillets of mackerel** and mix together with **2 tbsp crème fraîche, salt, cayenne pepper** and **1 tsp lemon juice**. Use chilled ingredients. Tear **2 heads of cleaned and trimmed endive lettuce** into small pieces and toss with a dressing prepared with **4 tbsp white wine vinegar, 4 tbsp olive oil, salt** and **pepper**. Scoop out egg-shaped portions of the fish mixture and arrange on plates together with the tossed salad and **8 cherry tomatoes**.

Preparation time: approx. 15 min., per portion:
approx. 14 g P,
15 g F, 1 g C,
199 kcal

Halibut Steaks with Saffron Rice

Gently sauté 1 peeled and chopped onion in 1 tbsp hot butter. Add 200 g/7 oz long grain rice, ¼ tsp ground saffron, 1 tsp salt as well as 400 ml/14 fl oz water and cook for about 20 minutes. Sprinkle 4 halibut steaks (150 g/5 oz each) with 2 tbsp lemon juice and fry in 2 tbsp oil on both sides for 4 minutes. Season with salt and pepper. Serve with the saffron rice and herb butter.

Preparation time: approx. 20 min., per portion: approx. 34 g P, 6 g F, 41 g C, 360 kcal

Fried Fish with Capers

Brush **4 coley fillets (about 600 g/1 lb 5 oz)** with **2 tbsp olive oil** and fry in a pan on both sides for about 2 minutes. Mix **16 sage leaves** together with **4 tbsp each of lemon juice** and **olive oil**, add **2 tbsp drained capers**. Cut **200 g/7 oz green lettuce leaves** into mouth-sized pieces and add together with **4 peeled and grated carrots**, **4 tomatoes** cut into quarters and **2 shallots** in rings. Arrange on plates with the fish fillets and drizzle with the sage and caper mixture.

Preparation time: approx. 20 min., per portion:

approx. 30 g P, 13 g F, 7 g C, 267 kcal

Trout and Cucumber Salad

Peel and remove the seeds from **1 cucumber** and purée with **a little salt.**
Fold in **125 ml/5 fl oz stiffly whipped cream** and season according to taste
with **pepper, 1 generous pinch of cayenne pepper** and **the juice of
1 lemon**. Peel **1 another cucumber**, finely grate and fold into the sauce. Cut
4 smoked fillets of trout into diamond-shaped pieces. Add to the cucumber
salad. Wash **1 more cucumber**, pat dry and cut into thin slices. Arrange
around the plate edges and place the salad on top.

Preparation time: approx. 20 min., per portion: approx. 19 g P, 13 g F, 6 g C, 222 kcal

Salmon and Potato Salad with Horseradish

Allow **500 g/1 lb 2 oz boiled potatoes** to cool, peel, cut into slices and mix together with **1 bunch of cleaned and sorted sea purslane**. Mix together **225 g/8 oz sour cream, 1/2 bunch freshly chopped herbs, 25 g/1 oz freshly grated horseradish, salt** and **pepper** and pour over the potatoes and purslane. Arrange on plates. Briefly fry **350 g/12 oz thinly sliced salmon** on both sides for about 1 minute in **2 tbsp hot oil**. Place on top of the salad and serve.

Preparation time: approx. 30 min., per portion: approx. 21 g P, 14 g F, 23 g C, 307 kcal

Soused Herring Salad with Melon

Cut **4 soaked soused herrings** into strips. Peel **1 Galia melon**, remove the seeds and dice. Mix the ingredients together with a mixture of **100 g/ 3½ oz crème fraîche, 1 tbsp lemon juice, 2 tbsp chopped dill, salt** and **pepper**. Fold in the torn leaves of **½ curly endive lettuce** and serve.

Preparation time: approx. 20 min., per portion: approx. 10 g P, 19 g F, 4 g C, 226 kcal

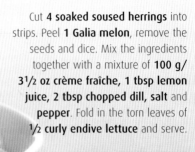

Baked Herrings

Remove the backbones from **800 g/1¾ lb cleaned and ready-to-cook fresh herrings**, sprinkle inside with **lemon juice** and **salt** and brush outside with **1 tbsp mustard**. Fill with **2 onions** cut into rings and fold together. Coat the herrings in **flour**, pressing down slightly, and place in a greased ovenproof dish.

Top with **2 tbsp butter flakes** and bake in the oven for about 25 minutes at 225°C/440°F/Gas 7 (fan oven 200°C/390°F/Gas 6). Serve with **boiled potatoes** and **vegetables**.

Preparation time: approx. 15 min., per portion: approx. 37 g P, 15 g F, 2 g C, 290 kcal

Poached Trout

Bend head-to-tail **4 ready-to-cook trout**, tie the head and tail together with kitchen string. Bring **250 ml/9 fl oz water** with **6 tbsp white wine vinegar** to the boil, pour over the trout. Bring to the boil **250 ml/9 fl oz white wine, 2 l/3½ pints water, 1 bay leaf, 4 tsp salt, 10 peppercorns** and **2 sprigs of parsley**, place the fish into the liquid and leave to stand for about 15 minutes. Whip **8 tbsp cream** until stiff and mix together with **2 tsp grated horseradish, sugar** and **salt**. Serve the trout with the creamed horseradish and **slices of lemon** and accompanied by **boiled potatoes**.

Preparation time: approx. 15 min.,

per portion: approx. 32 g P,

5 g F, 11 g C,

265 kcal

Haddock in Lobster Sauce

Sprinkle **4 haddock fillets** with **2 tbsp lemon juice**, heat up **400 ml/ 14 fl oz fish stock** with **100 ml/3¹/₂ fl oz white wine**, stir in **2 packets of white sauce mix** and bring to the boil. Cook the fish fillets in the sauce for about 10 minutes. Stir in **2 tsp lobster paste** and season with **salt** and **pepper**. Serve sprinkled with **3 tbsp chopped dill**. Boiled potatoes go well with this dish.

Preparation time: approx. 20 min., per portion: approx. 32 g P, 4 g F, 11 g C, 231 kcal

Asparagus with Prawns

6 dried shiitake mushrooms • 250 g/9 oz carrots • 750 g/
1 lb 10 oz green asparagus • salt • 3 tbsp sesame oil •
2 garlic cloves • 1 red chilli • 200 ml/7 fl oz chicken stock •
3 tbsp oyster sauce • 150 g/5 oz peeled prawns • pepper

Soak the mushrooms in warm water for about 10 minutes.
In the meantime, scrape the carrots and cut into sticks, peel the
lower third of the asparagus spears and cut diagonally into pieces.
Blanch the asparagus in boiling salted water for 5 minutes. Drain
off the soaking water from the mushrooms, remove the hard
stalks and cut the mushroom caps into strips.
Heat up the oil in a wok. Peel and dice the garlic. Trim the chilli,
remove the seeds and finely chop. Briefly sauté both in the hot
oil. Add the drained asparagus, mushrooms and carrot sticks and
stir-fry all the ingredients together for 3 minutes. Pour in the
chicken stock and oyster sauce and bring to the boil. Add the
prawns and cook together for 3 minutes. Season according to
taste with salt and pepper. Serve with rice.

Preparation time: approx. 20 min., per portion: approx. 18 g P, 6 g F, 33 g C, 233 kcal

TIP
If you wish, you can enhance this savoury spring dish
with roasted peanuts or cashew nuts. You can also add
fried strips of fish to the asparagus instead of the prawns.

Baked Fish with Tomatoes

Cut **1 kg/2¼ lb Thai catfish fillets** into chunks, drizzle with **the juice of 1½ lemons** and rub with **½ tsp each of salt, pepper** and **paprika**. Place in a greased casserole dish. Remove the stalk cores from **6 tomatoes**, slice and place on top of the fish. Sweat **1 peeled and chopped onion** in **3 tbsp hot olive oil**, add **2 peeled and chopped garlic cloves** with **1 chopped bunch mixed herbs**, **1 tbsp capers** and **¼ tsp rosemary** and sauté for 5 minutes. Pour the mixture over the sliced tomato and bake the casserole in the oven for about 15 minutes at 225°C/440°F/Gas 7 (fan oven 200°C/390°F/Gas 6).

Preparation time: approx. 15 min.,
per portion: approx. 47 g P, 6 g F, 6 g C,
280 kcal

Fish Casserole
with Potatoes

Peel and slice **400 g/14 oz potatoes** and
200 g/7 oz carrots. Cut **1 leek** into rings. Rub
4 fillets of hake with **salt** and cut into large chunks.
Grease a casserole dish and layer alternately with pieces of fish, potato
slices, carrot and leek. Drizzle with **2 tbsp oil** and pour in **100 ml/3¹/₂ fl oz
vegetable stock**.
Sprinkle the casserole with **1 bunch of chopped dill**, **salt** and **pepper** and
bake in the oven for about 35 minutes at 175°C/350°F/Gas 4 (fan oven
155°C/310°F/Gas 2). Serve with **200 g/7 oz sour cream** mixed with
1 tbsp tomato purée.

Preparation time: approx. 25 min., per portion: approx. 33 g P, 9 g F, 20 g C, 308 kcal

Spring Plaice

Gently sauté **4 chopped shallots** in **3 tbsp heated oil**, add **1 peeled cucumber** cut into chunks and cook together until done. Season with **salt** and **pepper**. Add **2 tbsp white wine vinegar** and cook until almost boiled away. Stir in **2 diced tomatoes** and keep the vegetables warm. Heat **3 tbsp butter** together with **1 tbsp oil** in a pan and fry **4 ready-to-cook young unskinned plaice** for 4 minutes on the one side, turn over and fry for 2 minutes on the other side. Season with **salt** and **pepper**. Drizzle the plaice with **a little lime juice.** Serve with the vegetables and garnished with **slices of lime.**

Preparation time: approx. 25 min., per portion: approx. 45 g P, 22 g F, 8 g C, 415 kcal

Grilled Swordfish

Prepare a marinade from **1 diced onion, 1 bunch of chopped dill** and **chervil, 4 tbsp oil** and **2 tbsp lemon juice**, pour over **4 swordfish steaks (250 g/9 oz each)** and leave to stand for about 1 hour.
Remove the fish from the marinade, drain and grill each side for about 4 minutes under a hot grill. Serve with **stir-fried vegetables** and **chopped thyme**.

Preparation time: approx. 15 min., per portion: approx. 50 g P, 15 g F, 1 g C, 392 kcal

Pike in Chervil Sauce

Cut **750 g/1 lb 10 oz fillet of zander pike** into chunks and drizzle with **the juice of 1 lemon**.
Sweat **2 peeled and chopped shallots** and **2 tbsp chopped chervil** in **2 tbsp butter** until translucent. Pour in **125 ml/4 fl oz fish stock** and **125 ml/ 4 fl oz cream** and reduce by a third. Cut **1 peeled carrot** into thin strips. Fry the chunks of fish on all sides in **3 tbsp hot butter** for about 3 minutes, cook with the strips of carrot. Stir **1 egg yolk** into the chervil sauce and whisk until creamy. Stir in **50 g/1¾ oz butter** in flakes. Season to taste and round off with **2 tbsp chopped chervil**. Serve with the fish and carrots.

Preparation time: approx. 25 min., per portion: approx. 39 g P, 15 g F, 5 g C, 325 kcal

Fillet of Trout with Wild Garlic Dip

Mix together **1 bunch of freshly chopped wild garlic, 200 g/7 oz sour cream, 75 g/2½ oz yoghurt** as well as **2 tbsp cream**. Season according to taste with **salt, pepper, sugar** and **grated lemon peel**. Butter **4 slices of wholemeal black bread**. Top with **4 smoked fillets of trout** and serve with the wild garlic dip.

Preparation time: approx. 20 min., per portion: approx. 22 g P, 20 g F, 19 g C, 352 kcal

Shrimp Salad with Chayote

Boil together **100 ml/3½ fl oz orange juice** and **50 ml/1¾ fl oz fresh lime juice** until reduced by half.

Leave to cool, then stir in **175 ml/6 fl oz vegetable oil** and season according to taste with **salt** and **pepper**. Arrange **200 g/7 oz cut-up mixed green lettuce leaves** in a bowl. Place **2 chayotes**, peeled and cut into thin strips, on top of the lettuce. Add **225 g/8 oz cooked shrimps** with the veins removed and sprinkle with **2 tbsp drained capers**.

Pour the dressing over the salad. Serve sprinkled with **2 tbsp freshly chopped dill** and garnished with **lemon wedges**.

Preparation time: approx. 30 min., per portion: approx. 12 g P, 14 g F, 10 g C, 216 kcal

Warm Shrimp Salad

Sauté **450 g/1 lb peeled shrimps** in **1 tbsp hot oil** until pink. Remove from the heat, add to the pan **2 chopped spring onions, 2 chopped garlic cloves** and **2 tsp ground ginger** and brown while shaking the pan. Allow to cool down a little. Arrange on plates the leaves of **2 heads of chicory** and the leaves of **1 head of radicchio** and **1 head of lettuce**. Coat with a dressing prepared with **50 ml/1¾ fl oz dry sherry, 3 tbsp lemon juice, 3 tbsp olive oil, ½ tsp chopped rosemary, salt** and **pepper**. Spoon the shrimps and onion mixture over the salad. Top with **200 g/7 oz red and yellow cherry tomatoes** cut in half and serve sprinkled with **2 tbsp roasted sesame seeds**.

Preparation time: approx. 25 min., per portion: approx. 3 g P, 8 g F, 6 g C, 207 kcal

Squid Salad

Cook **750 g/1 lb 10 oz ready-to-cook squid** together with **2 onions** cut into quarters, **1 bay leaf**, **1 tsp peppercorns**, salt, **2 tbsp lime juice** and **1 tsp coriander** in a pan with some water for about 30–40 minutes. Drain and cut into rings. Skin **1 beef tomato**, remove the seeds and dice, dice **1 cucumber** and mix both together with the squid rings. Mix **4 tbsp red wine vinegar** with **5 tbsp olive oil** and pour over the salad. Season with **salt** and **pepper**. Fold in **80 g/3 oz sliced stuffed green olives**. Serve on **lettuce leaves** sprinkled with **2 tbsp chopped parsley**.

Preparation time: approx. 30 min., per portion: approx. 31 g P, 11 g F, 8 g C, 260 kcal

Norway haddock with Asparagus and Dill

Peel **750 g/1 lb 10 oz white asparagus**, cut off the ends and cook in lightly salted water with **a little sugar** and **1 tsp butter** for about 12 minutes.
Place **4 Norway haddock fillets (120 g/4 oz each)** with **2 tbsp hot butter** in some water, bring to the boil and remove from the heat. Peel **1 carrot**, cut into strips and blanch.
Heat the drained asparagus in a frying pan together with the carrot strips, a little stock from cooking the fish and **1 bunch of chopped dill**, season according to taste with **salt** and **pepper**. Mix together **150 ml/5 fl oz stiffly whipped cream** and **1 egg yolk,** add to the pan and heat up.
Serve the fish with the asparagus and dill.

Preparation time: approx. 35 min., per portion: approx. 28 g P, 16 g F, 6 g C, 285 kcal

Fish Curry with Coriander

750 g/1 lb 10 oz filleted halibut · juice of 1 lemon ·
2 onions · 1 garlic clove · 1 tbsp butter · ½ bunch of freshly
chopped coriander · 1 tsp turmeric · 2 tbsp curry powder ·
1 tbsp coconut milk · 6 tomatoes · 150 g/5 oz yoghurt ·
salt · pepper

Cut the fish fillet into bite-sized chunks and drizzle with the
lemon juice. Peel the onions and garlic and finely chop. Heat the
butter in a saucepan and sweat the onions and garlic until
translucent. Add the coriander and spices as well as the coconut
milk and gently cook together for 3 minutes. Skin the tomatoes,
remove the stalk cores and seeds, cut in half and add to the pan.
Gently cook everything together for a further 5 minutes. Stir in
the yoghurt and heat up. Add the fish chunks to the sauce, cover
with a lid and cook for about 10 minutes. Season with salt and
pepper according to taste. Rice goes well with this dish.

Preparation time: approx. 15 min., per portion: approx. 40 g P, 6 g F, 8 g C, 260 kcal

TIP

You can make this mild curry a little hotter by
stirring in 1 tbsp green or yellow curry paste. You
can also substitute chicken or beef for the fish.

Steamed Norway Haddock

Drizzle **4 fillets of Norway haddock** with **2 tbsp lemon juice,** season with **salt** and **pepper**. Place in **2 tbsp hot oil** and **1 tsp hot butter**. Sprinkle on top with **1 yellow** and **1 green pepper**, both cut into strips, and **2 peeled and chopped garlic cloves**. Cover with a lid and steam in their own juices over a low heat for about 15 minutes. Spread **2 tbsp sour cream** mixed together with **1 bunch of freshly chopped parsley, 1 tsp cayenne pepper** and **1 dash Worcester sauce** over the fish and serve. This dish tastes delicious with **boiled potatoes**.

Preparation time: approx. 15 min., per portion: approx. 31 g P, 11 g F, 14 g C, 287 kcal

Fish Soup

Clean and trim **2 bunches of soup vegetables**, peel and dice if necessary. Sauté in **3 tbsp hot butter**. Pour in **1 l/1³/₄ pints fish or chicken stock** and simmer for 7 minutes. Cut **500 g/1 lb 2 oz filleted fish** into bite-sized pieces, drizzle with **2 tbsp vinegar** and leave to stand for 5 minutes. Then pat dry and cook in the soup for 3 minutes. Season with **salt, pepper, 2 peeled and crushed garlic cloves** and **1 bunch of chopped dill**.

Preparation time: approx. 15 min., per portion: approx. 25 g P, 4 g F, 3 g C, 155 kcal

Salad with Scallops

Cook **150 g/5 oz mountain lentils** for 20 minutes in plenty of boiling salted water together with **1 shallot spiked with 2 cloves, 1 garlic clove, 1 bay leaf, 2 sprigs thyme** and **6 stalks of parsley.** Drain and allow to cool. Sauté **1 peeled and diced bunch soup vegetables** in **2 tbsp hot butter** together with **40 g/ 1½ oz diced smoked bacon** and **2 chopped spring onions**. Mix together with the lentils, **salt, pepper, 2 tbsp balsamic vinegar** and **4 tbsp olive oil.** Season **12 scallops** and fry on both sides for about 5 minutes in **2 tbsp olive oil**. Serve with the salad and sprinkled with **parsley**.

Preparation time: approx. 40 min., per portion:
approx. 29 g P, 10 g F, 33 g C, 343 kcal

Spicy Mussel Salad

Cook **2 kg/4 lb 8 oz cleaned mussels** in **250 ml/9 fl oz white wine** until the shells open. Throw away any unopened shells, allow the mussels to cool in a bowl then remove from the shells. Mix together with the mussels **1 bulb fennel** cut into strips and **1 onion** cut into rings. Prepare a dressing with **5 tbsp white wine vinegar**, **1/2 tsp lemon juice**, **1/2 chopped clove of garlic**, **1/2 chopped red chilli**, **1/2 tsp ground fennel**, **salt** and **pepper** and pour over the salad. Serve garnished with **2 tbsp freshly chopped parsley**.

Preparation time: approx. 30 min., per portion: approx. 26 g P, 4 g F, 14 g C, 235 kcal

Poached Fish with Mustard Sauce

1/2 bunch spring onions · 500 ml/18 fl oz vegetable or fish stock · 5 white peppercorns · salt · 4 fish fillets (e.g. cod) · 1/2 bunch mixed herbs · 1 tbsp sugar · 2 tbsp malt vinegar · 2 tbsp mild mustard · 7 tbsp sunflower oil · pepper

Chop the spring onions into rings and bring to the boil in the vegetable or fish stock together with the peppercorns and a little salt and simmer for about 10 minutes. Place the fish fillets in a saucepan. Pour the liquid over the fish through a sieve and simmer for about 8 minutes.

Finely chop the herbs. Mix together the sugar, malt vinegar, mustard and herbs and dribble the sunflower oil into the mixture drop by drop. Mix well together and season according to taste with salt and pepper. Serve the fish fillets with the sauce and accompanied by boiled potatoes.

Preparation time: approx. 20 min., per portion: approx. 26 g P, 4 g F, 2 g C, 145 kcal

TIP

To prepare a conventional mustard sauce, use a béchamel sauce and enhance it with 2–3 tbsp medium-hot mustard.

Fish Goulash with Cucumber

Lightly sauté **2 peeled and chopped onions** in **1 tbsp butter**. Peel and remove the seeds from **2 cucumbers**, cut into 2 cm/³⁄₄ in chunks, add to the onions and briefly sauté together. Sprinkle with **2 tbsp flour**, sweat, pour in **250 ml/9 fl oz vegetable stock**, then stir in **125 g/4¹⁄₂ oz sour cream** and **2 tbsp mustard**.

Season the vegetables according to taste with **salt, pepper** and **a little sugar**.

Cut **400 g/14 oz coley fillets** into strips. Season, drizzle with **1 tbsp lemon juice** and cook in the cucumber mixture for 4 minutes. Sprinkle with **1¹⁄₂ bunches of freshly chopped dill** and serve with **creamed potatoes**.

Preparation time: approx. 25 min., per portion: approx. 20 g P, 21 g F, 5 g C, 297 kcal

Fish Salad with Cucumber

Allow **450 g/1 lb filleted Norway haddock** to stand for 5 minutes in a boiling marinade of **1 tbsp wine vinegar, 2 chopped onions, 1 bay leaf** and **salt**. Remove and flake the fish into small pieces. Mix together with **50 g/ 1³/₄ oz diced gherkins, 100 g/3¹/₂ oz diced cucumber, 10 sliced black olives** and **4 tomatoes cut** into wedges. Prepare a dressing with **1 tbsp light soy sauce, 1 tbsp tomato purée, 2 tbsp gherkin brine, 2 tbsp oil, salt** and **pepper** and mix into the salad.

Preparation time: approx. 20 min., per portion: approx. 23 g P, 16 g F, 5 g C, 260 kcal

Thai Catfish with Asparagus Salad

Peel **1 kg/2¹/₄ lb white asparagus**, cut off the ends, cut the spears into thin slices, leave the tips whole. Shell **300 g/11 oz fresh peas** and blanch in boiling salted water for about 5 minutes. Strain and allow to drain. Prepare a dressing with **1 chopped onion, 4 tbsp white wine vinegar, 6 tbsp olive oil, salt** and **pepper** and mix with the asparagus and peas. Leave to stand for 30 minutes. Season **600 g/1 lb 5 oz Thai catfish fillets**, dust with **flour** and coat in **2 beaten eggs** and **50 g/1³/₄ oz breadcrumbs** one after another. Fry on both sides in **3 tbsp hot oil** until golden brown. Cut into strips and arrange on top of the salad. Serve sprinkled with **chopped dill**.

Preparation time: approx. 30 min., per portion: approx. 42 g P, 5 g F, 26 g C, 325 kcal

Asparagus and Scampi Salad

Cut off the tips of **1.5 kg/3 lb 5 oz cleaned and trimmed green asparagus** and cook for about 3 minutes in boiling water with **salt** and a little **sugar**. Strain, catching the cooking water, and rinse in iced water. Cook the rest of the asparagus in 250 ml/9 fl oz of the cooking water for 5 minutes, blend to a purée and mix together with **1/2 tsp mustard, 2 tbsp vinegar, 50 ml/ 1³/4 fl oz oil, salt** and **pepper**. Pour the sauce over the asparagus tips and arrange on plates. Fry **12 ready-to-cook scampi** on all sides for about 1 minute in **4 tbsp olive oil**. Lay on top of the salad. Serve sprinkled with **2 tbsp freshly chopped chervil**.

Preparation time: approx. 30 min.,
per portion: approx. 18 g P, 9 g F, 6 g C, 178 kcal

Sweet and Sour Fish with Spring Vegetables

Cook **150 g/5 oz basmati rice** according to the instructions on the packet in boiling water for about 15 minutes. Cut **400 g/14 oz Norway haddock** into chunks. Whisk together **1 tbsp flour** and **1 egg** and season. Pour over the fish chunks. Heat **3 tbsp peanut oil** in a wok and fry the fish chunks until golden brown. Allow to drain. Add to the wok **½ peeled and diced cucumber, 150 g/5 oz drained canned pineapple chunks, ½ bunch spring onions** cut into rings and **200 g/7 oz scraped and sliced carrot**. Season with **1 tbsp brown sugar, 2 tbsp white wine vinegar** and **2 tbsp soy sauce** and fry for about 4 minutes. Add the fish chunks and heat through. Serve with the **basmati rice**.

Preparation time: approx. 20 min.,
per portion: approx. 24 g P, 8 g F,
44 g C, 355 kcal

Stuffed Plaice Rolls

Season **4 plaice fillets (750 g/1 lb 10 oz)** with **salt** and **pepper** and sprinkle with **2 tbsp lemon juice**. Lightly sauté **400 g/14 oz oyster mushrooms** cut into strips in **3 tbsp hot butter**. Simmer together with **1 chopped shallot** for 5 minutes, add **2 tbsp fish stock** and cook until almost boiled away. Stir in **200 g/7 oz crème fraîche** and season everything according to taste with **salt, pepper** and **lemon juice**. Simmer for another 5 minutes. From **1 bunch rocket** place 2 leaves on each fish fillet, roll up and secure with cocktail sticks. Place the fish rolls on top of the mushrooms cover with a lid and cook over a moderate heat for about 10 minutes. Serve the rest of the rocket leaves cut into strips together with the mushroom ragout and fish rolls.

Preparation time: approx. 20 min., per portion: approx. 39 g P, 23 g F, 4 g C, 387 kcal

Shrimp Cocktail

300 g/11 oz peeled shrimps • 1 tbsp lemon juice • 150 g/
5 oz lamb's lettuce • 200 g/7 oz canned mandarin oranges •
200 g/7 oz oyster mushrooms • 2 tbsp oil • 100 g/3$^{1}/_{2}$ oz
canned mung bean sprouts • 10 tbsp spicy ketchup • 6 tbsp
sour cream • 2 tbsp olive oil • salt • pepper • $^{1}/_{2}$ tsp paprika
powder • 4 leaves lollo rosso

Place the rinsed shrimps in a bowl and sprinkle with the lemon
juice. Clean and sort the lamb's lettuce, drain the mandarin oranges.
Clean the oyster mushrooms and cut into pieces. Stir-fry in the
hot oil for 3 minutes. Drain the bean sprouts. Add the salad ingredients to the shrimps. Mix together the ketchup, sour cream, olive
oil and seasoning and pour over the salad. Arrange on lollo
rosso leaves.

Preparation time: approx. 25 min., per portion: approx. 18 g P, 9 g F, 15 g C, 217 kcal

TIP
Try making this refreshing salad
with crayfish or large prawns.

Mediterranean Fish Kebabs

Cut **40 g/1½ oz cod fillet** into bite-sized pieces. Remove the veins from **8 peeled king prawns**. Cut **1 courgette** into 1 cm/⅓ in slices. Thread the ingredients together with **16 cocktail tomatoes** onto 8 wooden skewers. Prepare a marinade with **1 crushed garlic clove, 4 tbsp olive oil, salt, pepper** and **1 tsp Italian herbs** and use to brush the fish kebabs. Place the kebabs on a baking tray lined with aluminium foil and cook for about 8 minutes under a preheated grill at 250°C/480°F/Gas 9. Turn the kebabs several times and baste with the oil marinade.

Preparation time: approx. 15 min., per portion: approx. 38 g P, 7 g F, 3 g C, 236 kcal

Prawn Salad with Bean Sprouts

Blanch **350 g/12 oz soy bean sprouts** in boiling water for 30 seconds, strain and rinse in iced water. Allow to cool. Pluck **1 bunch watercress** and mix the leaves together with the bean sprouts, **16 large cooked prawns** and **2 tbsp roasted sesame seeds**. Stir together **2 tbsp soy sauce, 1 tbsp rice wine, 1 tbsp vinegar, 1 tbsp sesame oil, salt, pepper** and **honey** according to taste and pour over the salad. Mix together well and serve.

Preparation time: approx. 20 min., per portion: approx. 34 g P, 6 g F, 8 g C, 223 kcal

Salmon in Herb and Mustard Cream

800 g/1¾ lb filleted salmon • 1 tbsp lemon juice • salt •
pepper • 1 bunch each of dill, chives and parsley • 150 g/
5 oz crème fraîche • 5 tbsp fish stock • 2 tsp mustard

Sprinkle the filleted salmon with lemon juice. Season with salt
and pepper and place in an ovenproof dish. Rinse the herbs,
shake dry and finely chop. Mix ¾ of the herbs with the crème
fraîche, the stock and the mustard and spoon over the fish.
Bake the salmon in the oven for about 20 minutes at 200°C/
390°F/Gas 6 (fan oven 180°C/355°F/Gas 4). Serve sprinkled with
the remaining herbs.

Preparation time: approx. 10 min., per portion: approx. 38 g P, 24 g F, 2 g C, 382 kcal

TIP

This dish is also delicious with coley or Thai
catfish fillets instead of salmon. You can serve it
accompanied by rice or boiled potatoes.

338

Fish Salad

Fry **500 g/1 lb 2 oz coley fillet** cut into chunks in **10 g/1/3 oz hot butter** together with **1 chopped onion** for about 7 minutes in a pan with the lid on. Season with **salt**. Mix together **1/4 diced cucumber, 2 cored and diced apples** and **1/4 peeled and grated celeriac root**. Add the cooled fish together with **2 chopped hard-boiled eggs**. Fold into the salad **100 g/3½ oz salad cream** with **½ tsp curry powder, salt** and **pepper**. Serve garnished with **½ bunch of chopped parsley**.

Preparation time: approx. 30 min., per portion: approx. 29 g P, 20 g F, 14 g C, 350 kcal

Seafood Salad with Lemon Dressing

Cook **450 g/1 lb diced haddock, 2 fresh scallops, 225 g/8 oz diced fille- ted hake, 175 g/6 oz cleaned squid** cut into rings and **175 g/6 oz peeled prawns** in lightly salted boiling water for about 10 minutes. Strain and leave to cool. Mix together **6 tbsp freshly chopped parsley, 2 tbsp freshly chopped coriander, 4 tbsp freshly chopped mint, 3 tbsp olive oil** and the juices of both **1 lemon** and **1 lime** and season according to taste with **salt** and **pepper**. Pour over the seafood and leave to stand for 30 minutes.

Preparation time: approx. 30 min., per portion: approx. 52 g P, 12 g F, 7 g C, 348 kcal

Pasta,
Rice and
Potatoes

Penne with Capers and Anchovies

Boil **400 g/14 oz penne** until al dente. Cut **500 g/1 lb 2 oz peeled yellow peppers** into strips. Finely chop **12 anchovies**.
Crush **2 garlic cloves** and gently fry the vegetables in **3 tbsp heated olive oil**. Add **2 tbsp drained capers**, **1 tbsp each of freshly chopped basil** and **mint,** and season according to taste with **salt** and **pepper**.
Drain the pasta well. Fold into the vegetables, add **3 tbsp olive oil**, heat everything for a further 2 minutes then serve.

Preparation time: approx. 20 min., per portion: approx. 18 g P, 19 g F, 73 g C, 45 kcal

Pasta Salad with Roasted Vegetables

Place **4 2.5 cm/3 in slices of pumpkin, 2 courgettes** cut in half, **1 aubergine** and **1 red pepper**, both cut in half, on a greased baking tray and roast in the oven for about 40 minutes at 220°C/430°F/Gas 7 (fan oven 200°C/390°F/Gas 6). Turn several times.

Boil **175 g/6 oz spaghetti** until al dente. Remove the vegetables from the oven and leave to cool. Skin the pumpkin and pepper, cut the vegetables into small pieces. Mix together **6 tbsp olive oil, 2 tbsp balsamic vinegar, 1 tbsp mustard, salt, pepper** and **sugar** according to taste. Drain the pasta well. Mix with half the dressing. Layer the vegetables on top and pour the remaining dressing over them.

Preparation time: approx. 35 min., per portion: approx. 9 g P, 9 g F, 37 g C, 270 kcal

Baked Potatoes with Salmon Cream

Thoroughly wash **8 medium-sized new potatoes** and brush with **rapeseed oil**. Wrap in aluminium foil, lay on the oven rack and bake for about 40 minutes at 200°C/390°F/Gas 4 (fan oven 180°C/355°F/Gas 4). Dice **200 g/ 7 oz Salmon fillet** with the bones removed and mix together with **1 diced red onion**, **1/2 bunch of chopped chives**, **1 tbsp each of lemon juice and orange juice**, **1/2 tsp sweet paprika** and **1 tbsp rapeseed oil**. Cover with cling film and leave to stand in a cool place for about 1 hour. Then mix together with **125 g/4 1/2 oz cream cheese** and **1 tsp horseradish** from a jar and season according to taste with **salt** and **pepper**. Unwrap the potatoes, press open with a fork and top each one with a portion of the salmon cream. Sprinkle with **ground red peppercorns** and serve.

Preparation time: approx. 20 min., per portion: approx. 19 g P, 20 g F, 33 g C, 400 kcal

Oven Potatoes

Boil **4 large potatoes** in their skins for about 20 minutes. Strain the potatoes, allow the steam to dissipate, cut in half and place on a greased baking tray with the cut surface to the tray. Bake in the oven for about 15 minutes at 225°C/440°F/Gas 7 (fan oven 200°C/390°F/Gas 6).

Mix **1 bunch spring onions** chopped into rings together with **600 g/ 1 lb 5 oz finely diced drained tinned apricots**. Remove the seeds and finely chop **1 red chilli** and mix with **4 tbsp crème fraîche, salt** and **pepper**. Turn over the potatoes, spread with the apricot and onion mixture, top with some crème fraîche and season with pepper. Bake the potatoes for another 6 minutes. Serve warm garnished with **marjoram** and **thyme** leaves.

Preparation time: approx. 25 min., per portion: approx. 4 g P, 5 g F, 37 g C, 210 kcal

Pilaf with Fruit and Spring Onions

60 g/2 oz dried apricots with no added sulphur • juice of
1 orange • 2 spring onions • 200 g/7 oz strawberries • 2 tbsp
sunflower oil • 3 tbsp butter • 250 g/9 oz long grain rice •
5 tbsp raisins • 1/2 tsp ground cardamom • 1 tsp garam
masala • 1 tsp curry powder • 2 tbsp pistachios

Soak the dried apricots in orange juice for 5 minutes.
Chop the spring onions into fine rings. Quarter the strawberries.
Heat the oil and the butter in a pan and gently sauté the spring
onions while stirring. Add the rice and sweat until translucent.
Drain the apricots, cut into small pieces and add to the rice
together with the rinsed raisins. Stir the spices into the pilaf,
add the orange juice and 250 ml/9 fl oz water, cover with a
lid and cook over a low heat for 15–20 minutes until the rice
is done. Serve topped with the chopped pistachios.

Preparation time: approx. 30 min., per portion: approx. 6 g P, 8 g F, 66 g C, 380 kcal

TIP
Depending on the season, you can replace the
strawberries with peppers or use fresh apricots
instead of dried ones. You can also use grapes.

Ribbon Pasta Salad with Herbs

Boil **200 g/7 oz thin ribbon pasta** until al dente. Chop **1 bunch mixed herbs** and mix ⅔ of them with **100 g/3½ oz crème fraîche, 50 ml/ 1¾ fl oz cream** and **1 tbsp oil**. Season according to taste with **salt** and **pepper**. Drain the pasta well and mix together with **1 tbsp oil**, the remaining herbs, **salt** and **pepper**. Prepare **4 lettuce hearts** and cut into small pieces. Arrange the pasta salad on plates, top with the lettuce and drizzle with the herb dressing.

Preparation time: approx. 30 min., per portion: approx. 8 g P, 15 g F, 37 g C, 318 kcal

Wholemeal Pasta Salad

Boil **200 g/7 oz wholemeal pasta** in boiling salted water according to the directions on the packet. Drain well then mix together in a bowl with **1 tbsp butter, 1 chopped onion, 200 g/7 oz drained tinned sweet corn** and **200 g/7 oz drained tinned kidney beans**. Fold in **2 tomatoes** cut into eighths, **1 green pepper** cut into strips and **150 g/5 oz Emmental cheese** cut into thin strips. Mix together **50 g/1¾ oz sour cream, 150 g/5 oz yoghurt, 2 tbsp curry ketchup, 1 pinch paprika, salt, pepper, curry powder, 1 tbsp cranberry jelly** and **4 tbsp fruit vinegar**, pour over the salad and serve sprinkled with **3 tbsp chopped mixed herbs**.

Preparation time: approx. 30 min., per portion: approx. 20 g P, 18 g F, 25 g C, 348 kcal

Ravioli with Sage Butter

Prepare **400 g/14 oz fresh ravioli** from the refrigerated food section (with ricotta filling) according to the directions on the packet. Toss **8 fresh sage leaves** in **2 tbsp melted butter**. Season with **a little nutmeg**. Drain the ravioli, place in a bowl, coat with the sage butter and serve sprinkled with **100 g/3¹/₂ oz freshly grated Parmesan** and **pepper**.

Preparation time: approx. 15 min., per portion: approx. 29 g P, 14 g F, 21 g C, 337 kcal

Ribbon Pasta with Kohlrabi and Pesto

Boil **200 g/7 oz wholemeal ribbon pasta** together with **1 peeled kohlrabi** cut into chunks and **2 peeled carrots** cut into 3 cm/1 in pieces for about 8–10 minutes in boiling salted water. Then drain, retaining some of the cooking liquid. Mix **1 tbsp wild garlic pesto** with 2 tbsp of the cooking fluid, pour the mixture over the pasta in a pan and toss until evenly coated.

Preparation time: approx. 15 min., per portion: approx. 4 g P, 2 g F, 12 g C, 95 kcal

Stuffed Potatoes

Wash well **4–6 large potatoes** and prick with a fork. Place on a greased baking tray and bake in the oven for about 45 minutes at 200°C/390°F/ Gas 6 (fan oven 180°C/355°F/Gas 4).
Gently sauté while stirring **250 g/9 oz sliced mushrooms, 100 g/3½ oz soya bean sprouts** and **6 spring onions** cut into rings in **2 tbsp heated oil**, season with **salt** and **pepper**.
Cut off the upper third of the baked potatoes and scoop out some of the potato inside. Fill the cavity with the vegetable mixture and grill in the oven for about 10 minutes. Sprinkle with **50 g/1¾ oz freshly grated Parmesan** and **1 tsp dried thyme**.

Preparation time: approx. 20 min., per portion: approx. 10 g P, 20 g F, 28 g C, 337 kcal

Warm Potato Salad

Boil **800 g/1³/₄ lb potatoes** in their skins for about 20 minutes. Put **100 g/3¹/₂ oz finely-diced smoked bacon** in a hot pan. Sweat **2 shallots** cut into rings in the bacon fat until translucent. Pour in **150 ml/¹/₄ pint chicken stock**, bring to the boil and season according to taste with **2 tbsp white wine vinegar, salt** and **pepper**. Mix the drained, skinned and sliced potatoes with the mixture in the pan and leave to stand for 30 minutes. Heat up **100 ml/3¹/₂ fl oz chicken stock** with **4 tbsp olive oil** and pour over the salad. Season according to taste and serve immediately.

Preparation time: approx. 30 min., per portion: approx. 9 g P, 7 g F, 31 g C, 228 kcal

355

Fruity Rice Salad

Mix together **1 peeled and diced pear** sprinkled with **2 tbsp lemon juice, 150 g/5 oz halved black grapes, 150 g/5 oz cooked ham cut into strips** and **250 g/9 oz boiled rice.** Prepare a dressing with **the juice of ¹/₂ an orange, 1 tsp each of curry powder and chilli powder, 3 tbsp soy sauce, salt** and **pepper** and pour over the salad. Leave to stand for 1 hour. Arrange on a bed of **lettuce leaves**.

Preparation time:
approx. 20 min.,
per portion:
approx. 13 g P,
3 g F, 65 g C,
345 kcal

Tomato and Rice Salad

Gently sauté **1 chopped onion** and **1 chopped garlic clove** in **2 tbsp hot olive oil**. Skin and remove the seeds from **2 tomatoes**, dice, add to the pan and simmer for 5 minutes. Add **225 g/8 oz long grain rice** and **600 ml/ 1 pint water**, cover with a lid and cook for about 15–20 minutes. Drain the rice mixture well. Season according to taste with **salt, pepper** and **2 tbsp lemon juice**. Served sprinkled with **strips of basil**.

Preparation time: approx. 30 min.,

per portion: approx. 5 g P, 3 g F, 47 g C, 235 kcal

Pasta Salad with Turkey Breast

Boil **400 g/14 oz fusilli** until al dente. Meanwhile, gently sauté **1 chopped red onion** and **1 chopped garlic clove** in **2 tbsp hot olive oil**, add **200 g/7 oz sliced mushrooms, 50 g/1¾ oz peas** and **the juice of ½ lemon** and braise together for 2 minutes. Mix the drained pasta with the vegetables, **200 g/7 oz cooked turkey breast** cut into strips and **2 tbsp freshly chopped dill**. Season with **salt** and **pepper** according to taste, add about **125 ml/4 fl oz of the water** used to boil the pasta. Top with **150 g/5 oz halved cherry tomatoes** and serve sprinkled with **50 g/1¾ oz grated Parmesan**.

Preparation time: approx. 30 min.,
per portion: approx. 32 g P, 18 g F,
74 g C, 598 kcal

Glass Noodle Salad with Chilli

Pour boiling water over **400 g/14 oz glass noodles**, rinse in ice-cold water, and allow to drain. Mix the noodles together with **1 bunch spring onions** cut into rings, **1 bunch of chopped coriander, 2 freshly chopped red chillies, 1 chopped garlic clove, the juice of 2 limes, 5 tbsp oyster sauce, 2 tbsp sherry**, salt, pepper, sugar according to taste, and **3 tbsp sesame oil**. Allow the salad to stand for about 30 minutes.

Preparation time: approx. 15 min., per portion: approx. 7 g P, 5 g F, 37 g C, 227 kcal

Warm Pasta Salad with Chicken Strips

250 g/9 oz penne · 1 red onion · 1 garlic clove · 200 g/
7 oz mushrooms · 2 tbsp olive oil · juice of $1/2$ a lemon ·
100 g/$3^1/2$ oz frozen peas · 12 cherry tomatoes · 200 g/7 oz
cooked chicken · 50 g/$1^3/4$ oz Gouda cheese · 3 tbsp white
wine vinegar · salt · pepper · 2 tbsp freshly chopped herbs

Boil the penne in boiling salted water according to the instructions
on the packet until al dente. Peel the onion and garlic clove, slice
and chop respectively. Clean and trim the mushrooms, rub with a
damp cloth and cut into slices. Heat the oil in a pan and sweat the
onion, mushrooms and garlic until translucent. Add the lemon
juice and peas and braise for 4 minutes. Put to one side. Drain the
pasta, retaining 125 ml/$4^1/2$ fl oz of the cooking water. Place the
pasta in a bowl and mix together with the pea and mushroom
mixture. Fold in the halved cherry tomatoes, the chicken cut into
strips and the diced cheese, add the retained cooking water and
the vinegar. Season according to taste with salt and pepper. Serve
garnished with herbs.

Preparation time: approx. 30 min., per portion: approx. 27 g P, 7 g F, 50 g C, 382 kcal

TIP
To give the salad a more colourful appearance, use
coloured pasta, for example green red and white.
You can also use strips of turkey luncheon meat or
garlic sausage for the salad instead of chicken.

Tortellini Salad with Beetroot

Boil **250 g/9 oz tortellini** until al dente. Sweat **1 chopped onion** and **1 chopped garlic clove** in **1 tbsp hot oil** until translucent. Gently sauté together with **1 sliced yellow courgette** for 2 minutes. Season with **salt** and **pepper** and allow to cool. Mix the cooled vegetables together with **100 g/ 3½ oz drained beetroot** slices for a jar and season with **herb salt, pepper, 1 generous pinch cumin, ground clove** and **3 tbsp white balsamic vinegar**. Fold in the drained tortellini and leave to stand for 30 minutes.

Preparation time: approx. 20 min., per portion: approx. 9 g P, 4 g F, 47 g C, 260 kcal

Macaroni with Olive Paste

Boil **400 g/14 oz macaroni** according to the instructions on the packet until al dente. Drain well. Cut **75 g/2½ oz whole green olives with herbs** in half, remove the stones and purée together with **4 rinsed anchovy fillets in oil, 1 garlic clove** and **2 tbsp olive oil**. Stir together **2 tbsp olive oil, 1 tbsp lemon juice, 1 tsp Worcester sauce** and **1 tsp dried oregano** and mix with the olive paste. Season according to taste with **salt** and **pepper**.
Dice **500 g/1 lb 2 oz skinned beef tomatoes**, cut **200 g/7 oz artichoke hearts** from a jar into quarters. Gently sauté both in **2 tbsp hot olive oil** and season. Mix the macaroni with the vegetables and briefly heat. Serve immediately with the olive paste.

Preparation time: approx. 30 min., per portion: approx. 35 g P, 8 g F, 74 g C, 510 kcal

Oven Potatoes with Mixed Herb Sauce

Scrape **750 g/1 lb 10 oz new potatoes**, cut into wedges and place on a greased baking tray. Bake in the oven for about 20 minutes at 200°C/390°F/ Gas 6 (fan oven 180°C/355°F/Gas 4). Sprinkle with **herb salt** and **pepper**. Drizzle with **2 tbsp olive oil**. Finely chop **1–2 bunches of mixed green herbs**. Mix together with **300 g/11 oz sour cream, 1 pot of yoghurt, 2 chopped hard-boiled eggs, 2 chopped gherkins, 1 tsp mustard, 1 tbsp lemon juice, salt** and **pepper**. Serve the potatoes with the green herb sauce.

Preparation time: approx. 15 min., per portion: approx. 7 g P, 11 g F, 33 g C, 282 kcal

Potato and Cucumber Salad

Boil **750 g/1 lb 10 oz potatoes** in their skins for about 20 minutes. Peel **1 cucumber**, cut into thin slices, sprinkle with **1 tsp salt** and leave to stand for 20 minutes. Drain off the liquid. Strain the potatoes, skin and cut into slices. Mix together with the sliced cucumber in a bowl. Mix together **3 tbsp white wine vinegar, 2 tbsp oil, 50 g/1³/4 oz sour cream, salt, pepper** and **sugar** according to taste. Pour over the potato and cucumber salad, sprinkle with **ground red peppercorns** and serve garnished with **2 tbsp freshly chopped dill.**

Preparation time: approx. 20 min., per portion: approx. 5 g P, 4 g F, 30 g C, 180 kcal

Crunchy Vegetable Rice

250 ml/9 fl oz vegetable stock • 150 g/5 oz wholegrain rice •
1 cucumber • 1 bunch radishes • 3 carrots • 4 spring onions •
4 tbsp raspberry vinegar • Salt • lemon pepper • 5 tbsp
grape seed oil • 50 g/1¾ oz chopped mixed herbs

Bring the vegetable stock to the boil in a saucepan. Add the rice
and cook with the lid on over a low heat for about 40 minutes.
Rinse the cucumber and radishes thoroughly and slice finely. Peel
the carrots and cut into thin sticks. Chop the spring onions into
rings. Prepare a marinade with vinegar, salt, pepper, oil and the
mixed herbs and mix with the vegetables. Fold the vegetable
mixture into the strained rice and serve lukewarm garnished
with the leaves of the radishes.

Preparation time: approx. 35 min., per portion: approx. 6 g P, 8 g F, 39 g C, 255 kcal

TIP
Try out this tasty salad
with pasta or boiled grains
of corn instead of rice.

Linguine with Balsam Lentils

Boil **400 g/14 oz linguine** in boiling salted water until al dente. Gently sauté **1 trimmed leek** cut into rings and **1 peeled and chopped garlic clove** in **1 tbsp olive oil**. Add **530 g/1 lb 3 oz drained tinned lentils, 200 ml/7 fl oz vegetable stock** and **80 g/3 oz finely cut dried tomatoes**. Stir in **4 tbsp balsamic vinegar** and season with **salt** and **pepper**. Simmer the mixture for about 5 minutes. Spoon on top of the linguine and serve garnished with **cherry tomatoes**.

Preparation time:
approx. 20 min.,
per portion: approx. 21 g P,
6 g F, 87 g C, 505 kcal

Penne all'Arrabbiata with Peas

Boil **400 g/14 oz penne** in salted water until al dente. Add **300 g/11 oz defrosted frozen peas** to the pasta 2 minutes before the end of the cooking time. Drain everything well.

Blend **30 g/1 oz tomato purée, 1 tbsp ketchup, 1 crushed garlic clove, 2 tsp capers** and **2 tbsp olive oil** to a purée and season with **salt, pepper** and **1 pinch of sugar**. Stir **1 chopped red chilli** without the seeds into the purée. Mix the hot pasta and peas with the chilli sauce, **80 g/3 oz stoned black olives** and **½ bunch of chopped parsley** and top with **40 g/1½ oz shaved Parmesan**.

Preparation time: approx. 15 min., per portion: approx. 22 g P, 15 g F, 83 g C, 510 kcal

Spaghetti with Vegetable Sauce

Cut **5 peeled carrots** and **1 peeled kohlrabi** into sticks, cut **1/2 head of celery** into thin rings. Dice **1 courgette** and **8 tomatoes**. Gently fry the vegetables in **2 tbsp hot oil**. Season with **salt** and **pepper**. Add **1 tbsp tomato purée** and **300 ml/11 fl oz vegetable juice** and simmer for 15 minutes. Boil **400 g/14 oz spaghetti** according to the directions on the packet until al dente. Fold the drained spaghetti into the vegetable sauce and serve sprinkled with **50 g/1¾ oz freshly grated Parmesan** and **1 tbsp basil** cut into strips.

Preparation time: approx. 15 min., per portion: approx. 22 g P, 10 g F, 83 g C, 530 kcal

German Gnocchi

Boil **500 g/1 lb 2 oz peeled and diced potatoes** in boiling salted water for 10 minutes. Strain, allow to cool briefly and mix to a purée with **2 eggs, 4 tsp flour** and **2 tsp cornflour**. Season according to taste with **salt, pepper** and **nutmeg**. With floured hands, form finger-shaped gnocchi and cook in boiling salted water for 5 minutes until they float to the top. Remove, drain and toss in **50 g/1³⁄4 oz melted butter**. Serve to accompany meat, with sauerkraut or a salad.

Preparation time: approx. 20 min., per portion: approx. 7 g P, 14 g F, 25 g C, 265 kcal

Wild Rice Salad with Apricots

75 g/2^1/$_2$ oz wild rice mix · ^{1}/$_2$ medium-sized apple ·
^{1}/$_2$ green pepper · ^{1}/$_2$ stalk celery · 50 g/1^3/$_4$ oz dried
apricots · 2 tbsp soy sauce · 2 tsp sugar · 2 tsp fruit
vinegar · 25 g/1 oz roasted unsalted peanuts · lettuce
leaves to garnish

Boil the rice according to the instructions on the packet until al
dente. Strain and put on a plate to cool, turning repeatedly. Peel
and core the apple, remove the seeds from the pepper, clean
and trim the celery. Finely dice them all. Finely dice the apricots.
Place the diced fruit and vegetables in a bowl. Prepare a dressing with the soy sauce, sugar, fruit vinegar and 2 tbsp water and
fold into the fruit and vegetable mixture. Stir thoroughly and
serve garnished with the peanuts and lettuce leaves.

Preparation time: approx. 50 min., per portion: approx. 5 g P, 4 g F, 28 g C, 170 kcal

TIP
You can also enhance the salad
by adding 150 g/5 oz cooked
chicken or turkey breast.

Rice Salad with Curry

Sweat **1 chopped onion** in **1 tbsp butter** until translucent. Add **150 g/ 5 oz wholegrain rice** and **450 ml/16 fl oz vegetable stock** and cook for about 40 minutes. Drain off excess water, season with **salt, pepper** and **1 tsp curry powder**. Mix together **125 g/4½ oz sour cream, 1 crushed garlic clove, the juice of ½ lemon, 1 tsp mustard, 3 tbsp sunflower oil, salt** and **pepper**. Mix with the rice, leave to stand for 30 minutes. Fold in **150 g/5 oz peeled and grated celeriac, 1 tbsp chopped hazelnuts** and **50 g/1¾ oz alfalfa sprouts** and serve.

Preparation time: approx. 20 min., per portion: approx. 6 g P, 12 g F, 34 g C, 270 kcal

Wild Rice Salad

Boil **150 g/5 oz wild rice** in a covered saucepan with **300 ml/11 fl oz boiling water** for about 40 minutes. Strain and allow to cool slightly. Mix **200 g/7 oz skinned and diced tomatoes** with the seeds removed and **1 bunch of chopped basil** with a dressing prepared from **2 tbsp sour cream, 80 ml/3 fl oz cream, 1 tsp mustard, 1 tbsp lime juice, salt** and **pepper**. Mix with the wild rice. Serve on a bed of **lettuce leaves** garnished with **100 g/3½ cheese** cut into strips.

Preparation time: approx. 60 min., per portion: approx. 10 g P, 9 g F, 32 g C, 245 kcal

Spaghetti with Aubergines and Tomatoes

Cut **500 g/1 lb 2 oz cleaned and trimmed aubergines** into thin chunks
and brown well in **3 tbsp olive oil**. Add **2 peeled and chopped garlic
cloves** and fry together. Add **400 g/14 oz peeled and diced tomatoes**
with the seeds removed and braise for 5 minutes. Then crush with a fork.
Simmer the mixture for another 10 minutes.
Boil **300 g/11 oz spaghetti** according to the instructions on the packet until
al dente. Serve the drained pasta topped with the aubergine and tomato
mixture. Garnish with **basil** and **5 tbsp grated Parmesan.**

Preparation time: approx. 15 min., per portion: approx. 13 g P, 7 g F, 57 g C, 357 kcal

Ribbon Pasta with Mixed Peppers

Fry **100 g/3½ oz diced streaky bacon** in **1 tbsp oil**, add **1 peeled and chopped onion** and **1 peeled and chopped garlic clove** and sauté together. Add **1 red, 1 green** and **1 yellow pepper**, trimmed, with the seeds removed and diced, and cook together for 5 minutes. Meanwhile, boil **400 g/14 oz wholemeal ribbon pasta** in plenty of boiling salted water until al dente. Add **100 ml/3½ fl oz white wine** and **150 ml/5 fl oz vegetable stock** to the peppers mixture and reduce slightly. Stir in **salt, pepper** and **½ bunch each of chopped thyme** and **rosemary**. Finally, fold in **100 ml/ 3½ fl oz thickly whipped cream**. Serve the vegetables with the pasta.

Preparation time: approx. 20 min., per portion: approx. 12 g P, 18 g F, 25 g C, 330 kcal

Green Beans with Rice

500 g/1 lb 2 oz green beans · 2 onions · 200 g/7 oz rice ·
50 ml/1¾ fl oz olive oil · salt · 20 g/¾ oz butter · paprika

Trim the beans, wash and cut up into small pieces. Finely dice
the onions. Wash the rice and allow to drain. Heat the oil in a
saucepan and gently sauté the onions. Add the rice and briefly
sauté together in the olive oil. Pour in 400 ml/14 fl oz water, add
the beans and cook everything over a low heat until the rice is
done. After 5 minutes, add ½ tsp salt.
Melt the butter in a pan, stir in the paprika.
Place the drained rice and beans in a bowl and drizzle with the
paprika butter. Serve warm or cold.

Preparation time: approx. 20 min., per portion: approx. 7 g P, 17 g F, 45 g C, 363 kcal

TIP
If you wish, you can also stir in
2 tbsp herb vinegar and sprinkle
with 2 tbsp freshly chopped parsley.

379

Asparagus Risotto with Herbs

Boil **500 g/1 lb 2 oz asparagus** cut into 4 cm/1¹/2 in chunks for 5 minutes in 1.5 l/2¹/2 pints boiling salted water with **10 g/¹/3 oz butter** and **1 tsp sugar.** Remove and drain. Gently sauté **2 chopped shallots** in **3 tbsp oil,** add **200 g/7 oz Arborio rice** and **1 bay leaf** and stir to coat the rice in the oil. Separate 200 ml/7 fl oz from 700 ml/ 1¹/4 pints of the water used for cooking the asparagus, add to the rice and stir until absorbed. Gradually add the remaining cooking water a little at a time, after 10 minutes fold the asparagus chunks and **100 g/3¹/2 oz frozen peas** into the rice. When the rice is smooth and creamy, stir in **1 tbsp butter** and **2 tbsp each of chopped parsley** and **chervil**. Serve sprinkled with **20 g/³/4 oz grated Parmesan**.

Preparation time: approx. 30 min., per portion: approx. 9 g P, 9 g F, 46 g C, 313 kcal

Vegetable Risotto

Gently sauté **1 peeled and chopped onion** in **2 tbsp olive oil**. Add **200 g/ 7 oz risotto rice** and while stirring sweat for 2 minutes. Now gradually pour in **800 ml/1 pint 8 fl oz vegetable stock** a little at a time, just sufficient to cover the rice, and only top up when the liquid is completely absorbed. Gently sauté **2 spring onions** cut into rings and **2 leeks** also cut into rings in **1 tbsp hot oil**. Add **100 g/3¹⁄₂ oz frozen peas** and cook together while stirring. Add **50 g/1³⁄₄ oz sliced mushrooms**, pour in **150 ml/5 fl oz white wine** and reduce slightly. Season with **salt, pepper** and **1 tsp dried thyme**. Fold the vegetables into the creamy rice and serve.

Preparation time: approx. 30 min., per portion: approx. 7 g P, 6 g F, 47 g C, 282 kcal

Glass Noodle Salad with Red Pepper

Cut **200 g/7 oz beef** into strips and fry for about 1 minute in **2 tbsp hot vegetable oil.**
Fry together with **1 red pepper** cut in strips and **1 leek** cut into rings for 2 minutes. Add **75 g/2¹/₂ oz drained soaked glass noodles** and **1 chopped red chilli**. Briefly fry everything together, then pour into a bowl. Mix together, **4 tbsp rice wine vinegar, 2 tbsp sake, 4 tbsp oyster sauce, 2 tbsp chopped coriander, salt** and **pepper** and pour over the salad.

Preparation time: approx. 20 min., per portion: approx. 12 g P, 7 g F, 8 g C, 150 kcal

Pasta with Salmon and Rocket

Boil **175 g/6 oz spelt-flour macaroni** according to the instructions on the packet. Cut **250 g/9 oz wild salmon fillets** into thin strips and season with **salt, pepper** and **2 tbsp lemon juice**. Heat **1 tbsp butter** in a pan and gently sauté **1 peeled and chopped shallot**. Add the drained pasta and shake the pan to mix well. Pour in **200 ml/7 fl oz cream** and fold in the strips of salmon. Simmer over a low heat for 5 minutes. Season according to taste with **salt** and **pepper**.

Arrange on plates and garnish with **1 bunch of rinsed and sorted rocket leaves** and **50 g/1¾ oz Parmesan flakes**.

Preparation time: approx. 20 min., per portion: approx. 23 g P, 26 g F, 33 g C, 467 kcal

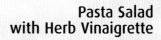

Pasta Salad with Herb Vinaigrette

Boil **250 g/9 oz spaghetti** until al dente. Mix together **100 g/3½ oz sliced cherry tomatoes**, **1 diced yellow pepper**, **4 stalks of celery** cut into thin rings, and **150 g/5 oz Alpine cheese** cut into strips. Drain the pasta and mix together with the vegetables. Prepare a dressing with **100 g/3½ oz finely chopped Italian herbs**, **4 tbsp white balsamic vinegar**, **4 tbsp olive oil**, **salt**, **pepper** and **paprika** and pour over the salad. Leave to stand for 10 minutes.

**Preparation time:
approx. 20 min.,
per portion: approx. 21 g P,
20 g F, 49 g C, 465 kcal**

Green Pasta Salad with Prawns

Peel **300 g/11 oz king prawns**, remove the veins, rinse well and pat dry. Leave to stand for about 1 hour in a marinade of **2 crushed garlic cloves, 4 tbsp orange juice, 4 tbsp olive oil** and **a little salt**. Boil **350 g/12 oz green spaghetti** until al dente. Drain well. Mix together **4 tbsp crème fraîche, 2 tbsp lemon juice, salt** and **pepper**. Fold in **1/2 bunch lemon balm leaves** cut into thin strips. Pat the prawns dry and fry in a pan on both sides for about 3 minutes. Mix the pasta together with the dressing in a bowl. Add the prawns and serve garnished with **lemon wedges**.

Preparation time: approx. 20 min., per portion: approx. 24 g P, 5 g F, 62 g C, 393 kcal

Warm Rice Salad

200 g/7 oz brown lentils • salt • 200 g/7 oz basmati rice •
1 bunch spring onions • 2 garlic cloves • 100 ml/3½ fl oz
olive oil • 2 tsp ground cinnamon • 2 tsp paprika • 2 tsp
ground cumin • pepper • 2 tbsp freshly chopped coriander

Soak the lentils overnight. Strain the next day, boil in salted water
for about 40 minutes. After 20 minutes of cooking, add the rice
and cook together.

Chop the spring onions into rings. Crush the garlic cloves. Heat the
oil and sweat both the onions and the garlic for about 5 minutes.
Add the spices and simmer everything for another 5 minutes.
Strain the rice and lentils well. Stir into the mixture in the
saucepan. Fold in the coriander and season according to taste
with salt and pepper. Serve warm.

Preparation time: approx. 30 min., per portion: approx. 9 g P, 14 g F, 51 g C, 362 kcal

TIP

Try out this rice salad with a mixture of wild
rice, wholegrain rice and red lentils. This
mixture is already available in some shops.

Potato Salad with Spring Onions

Boil **750 g/1 lb 10 oz potatoes** in their skins for 20 minutes. Bring to the boil **1 bunch spring onions** cut into rings and **250 ml/9 fl oz vegetable stock**, then remove from the heat. Mix into the stock **½ tbsp mustard, 2 tbsp white wine vinegar** and **4 tbsp sunflower oil**. Skin the cooled potatoes, cut into slices and mix with the warm dressing. Fold in **1 tbsp drained capers** and **150 g/5 oz endive lettuce** cut into strips.

Preparation time: approx. 25 min., per portion: approx. 5 g P, 7 g F, 30 g C, 203 kcal

Sweet Potato Salad with Dill

Boil **750 g/1 lb 10 oz sweet potatoes** in their skins for about 20 minutes. Drain well, remove the skins and dice. Prepare a dressing with **2 tbsp white wine vinegar, 2 tbsp cider vinegar, 1 tbsp brown sugar, salt, 1 tsp mustard, 150 g/5 oz yoghurt, 150 g/5 oz sour cream, 1 tbsp fresh lemon juice** and **½ bunch of freshly chopped dill** and mix together with the potatoes. Season according to taste with **salt, pepper** and **paprika** and serve.

Preparation time: approx. 30 min., per portion: approx. 6 g P, 7 g F, 50 g C, 290 kcal

Desserts

Kiwi Fruit Cocktail

Peel **8 kiwi fruit**, cut into thin slices. Peel **1 mango**, cut the fruit away from the stone in wedges. Remove the seeds from **¹/₂ cantaloupe melon**, scoop the fruit with a melon baller. Arrange the fruit in glasses. Sprinkle with **2 tbsp icing sugar** and **1 tbsp mint liqueur**. According to taste, fill up with **sparkling wine** or serve garnished with **whipped cream**.

Preparation time: approx. 20 min., per portion: approx. 1 g P, 1 g F, 19 g C, 108 kcal

Pineapple Salad

Peel **200 g/7 oz fresh pineapple**, dice and marinate in **3 tbsp sugar** and **20 ml/4 tsp Marsala** for 15 minutes. Mix **1 tbsp chopped almonds** and **3 tbsp coconut flakes** and mix together with **the juice of 1 orange**. Add the pineapple to the coconut flakes and mix together well. Serve garnished with **125 ml/4 fl oz whipped cream**.

Preparation time: approx. 20 min., per portion: approx. 2 g P, 13 g F, 15 g C, 182 kcal

Baked Apples

4 medium-sized cooking apples · 2 tbsp raisins ·
3 tbsp orange juice · 2 tbsp coarsely chopped hazelnuts ·
1 pinch cinnamon · 2 tbsp honey · fat for greasing the dish

Remove the cores of the apples with an apple corer.
Rinse the raisins under hot water, drain and soak in orange juice,
then drain again. Mix the hazelnuts together with the cinnamon,
honey and raisins. Place the apples in a greased ovenproof dish
and fill with the nut and raisin mixture. Bake in the oven for
about 30 minutes at 180°C/355°F/Gas 4 (fan oven 160°C/
320°F/Gas 3).

Preparation time: approx. 15 min., per portion: approx. 1 g P, 4 g F, 23 g C, 132 kcal

TIP
This is a wonderful dish for autumn and winter.
Baked apples taste even better when served
with vanilla sauce and a blob of cream.

Pineapple Cake

For about 9 slices

Mix together **210 g/7¹⁄₂ oz flour, 80 g/3 oz sugar** and **2 tsp baking powder.** Drain **225 g/8 oz tinned unsweetened pineapple chunks**, reserving the juice. Stir together **1 egg, 3 tsp melted butter, ¹⁄₂ tsp ground vanilla,**

2 tbsp brown sugar, 50 ml/1³⁄₄ fl oz low-fat milk, 40 ml/2¹⁄₂ tbsp pineapple juice, 10 ml/ 2 tsp white rum and the **pineapple chunks.** Add to the flour mixture and work together until smooth. Place the cake mixture into a greased baking tin (20 x 20 cm/8 x 8 in) and bake in the oven for about 30 minutes at 175°C/350°F/Gas 4 (fan oven 150°C/300°F/Gas 2). Decorate with **coconut flakes**.

Preparation time: approx. 30 min.,
per piece: approx. 3 g P, 3 g F, 33 g C, 180 kcal

Stuffed Pineapple

Cut **2 baby pineapples** with leaves in half, cut out the hard inner core and some of the fruit and finely dice the removed fruit.

Mix **100 g/3½ oz each of both prepared raspberries** and **prepared blackberries** together with **2 small peeled and sliced bananas** and sprinkle with **the juice of ½ lime**. Stir together **200 g/7 oz yoghurt** and **50 ml/1¾ fl oz coconut syrup**.

Add **40 ml/2½ tbsp white rum** to the fruit and use to fill the pineapple halves. Arrange on plates and coat with the coconut yoghurt. Serve sprinkled with **1 pinch cinnamon** and **a little desiccated coconut**.

Preparation time: approx. 25 min., per portion: approx. 3 g P, 2 g F, 35 g C, 200 kcal

397

Curd Cheese Waffles with Fruit

Mix together **125 g/4½ oz low-fat curd cheese, 60 g/2 oz melted butter, 3 tbsp sugar** and **the grated peel of 1 organic lemon**. Sieve in **150 g/5 oz flour**, stir in **125 ml/4 fl oz low-fat milk** and **3 egg yolks**. Whip **3 egg whites** until stiff, fold into the batter. Use a waffle iron to bake 8 waffles from the batter. Blend **350 g/12 oz raspberries, a little vanilla sugar** and **20 ml/4 tsp raspberry schnapps** to a purée. Fold in **200 g/ 7 oz curd cheese**. Spread the fruit cream over the waffles and serve.

Preparation time: approx. 25 min., per portion: approx. 11 g P, 9 g F, 21 g C, 228 kcal

Plum Salad

Blanch **500 g/1 lb 2 oz trimmed and sorted plums** in boiling water for 6 minutes. Drain and allow to cool. Skin the plums, cut in half and remove the stones. Cut **2 pieces of stem ginger** into thin strips and fold into the plums. Mix together **6 tbsp double cream, 20 ml/4 tsp plum schnapps, 2 tbsp icing sugar** and **1 generous pinch each of both cinnamon** and **ground ginger**. Place the fruit in a bowl, cover with the sauce and leave to stand for 30 minutes. Serve sprinkled with **freshly grated ginger**.

Preparation time: approx. 30 min.,
per portion: approx. 1 g P, 2 g F, 17 g C, 97 kcal

Buttermilk Waffles with Fruit Curd Cheese

Prepare a smooth batter with **100 g/3¹/₂ oz butter, 2 eggs, 150 g/5 oz flour** mixed with **¹/₂ tsp baking powder,** and **125 ml/4 fl oz buttermilk.** Mix together with **the seeds (scraped) from 1 vanilla pod** and **2 tbsp sugar** and leave to stand for 15 minutes.

Cut in half **150 g/5 oz each of black and green grapes** and mix with **200 g/7 oz drained tinned mandarin oranges.** Drizzle with **2 tbsp lemon juice** and **2 tbsp Noilly Prat** and leave to stand. Then mix together with **200 g/7 oz low-fat curd cheese.** Flavour according to taste with **vanilla sugar.** Use the batter to bake 8 waffles and serve with the fruit curd cheese.

Preparation time: approx. 40 min., per portion: approx. 8 g P, 12 g F, 26 g C, 253 kcal

Apple and Yoghurt Tart

For 12 slices

Beat **3 egg whites** with **3 tbsp cold water**, **100 g/3¹/₂ oz sugar** and **2 tsp vanilla sugar** until stiff. Stir in **3 egg yolks.** Sieve into the egg mixture **75 g/2¹/₂ oz each of both flour** and **cornflour** as well as **1 tsp baking powder** and fold in. Pour the mixture into a spring-form cake tin (26 cm/ 10¹/₂ in diameter) lined with baking paper and bake in the oven for about 20 minutes at 200°C/390°F/Gas 6 (fan oven 175°C/350°F/Gas 4). Leave to cool, then slice horizontally in two. Mix **375 g/13 oz low-fat curd cheese** with **375 g/13 oz yoghurt, 2 tsp vanilla sugar, 30 g/1 oz sugar** and **2 tsp dissolved gelatine powder.**

Fold in **100 ml/3¹/₂ fl oz stiffly whipped cream** as well as **350 g/ 12 oz apple sauce** (unsweetened if available). Allow to stand in a cool place. Spread the yoghurt and curd cheese mixture over the bottom half of the cake. Lightly cut diagonally across the top half to mark out where the portions are to be cut and place on top of the yoghurt mixture. Place in the fridge to set.

Preparation time: approx. 30 min., per slice: approx. 8 g P, 5 g F, 20 g C, 166 kcal

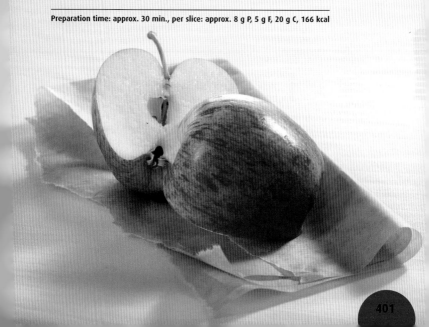

Elderberry Cake

For about 20 slices

Knead together **500 g/1 lb 2 oz puréed boiled potatoes, 400 g/14 oz flour, 50 g/1³/₄ oz cornflour, 2 eggs, 1 pinch salt, 100 g/3¹/₂ oz margarine** and **50 g/1³/₄ oz sugar** to a firm dough. Roll out on a floured worktop and use to line the bottom of a spring-form cake tin (28 cm/11¹/₂ in diameter), building up a lip around the edge. Spread **600 g/1 lb 5 oz prepared elderberries** over the dough and bake the cake in the oven for about 20 minutes at 200°C/390°F/Gas 6 (fan oven 180°C/355°F/Gas 4). Beat **2 eggs, 75 g/2¹/₂ oz sugar** and **200 g/7 oz sour cream** until foamy. Pour the mass over the cake and bake for a further 15 minutes.

Preparation time: approx. 30 min., per slice: approx. 4 g P, 6 g F, 25 g C, 174 kcal

Apricot Cake

For about 16 pieces

Drain **850 g/1 lb 14 oz tinned unsweetened apricots**. Whisk together
3 egg yolks, 6 tbsp lukewarm water and **100 g/3½ oz sugar** until foamy.
Beat **3 egg whites** with **1 pinch salt** until stiff and add to the egg cream
together with **1 tsp grated peel** of an untreated lime. Add **150 g/5 oz
wholemeal spelt** flour mixed with **1 tsp cream of tartar** and mix until
smooth. Pour the mixture into a spring-form cake tin (26 cm/10½ in
diameter) lined with baking paper. Place the apricot halves on top with the
cut surface to the cake mixture and bake in the oven for about 25 minutes
at 180°C/355°F/Gas 4 (fan oven 160°C/320°F/Gas 3). Allow to cool then
dust with **icing sugar**.

Preparation time: approx. 25 min., per piece: approx. 2 g P, 1 g F, 21 g C, 114 kcal

Mandarin Orange and Rice Cake

For about 12 pieces
370 g/12^1/$_2$ oz tinned mandarin oranges • 1 vanilla pod •
400 ml/14 fl oz low-fat milk • 100 g/3^1/$_2$ oz pudding rice •
50 g/1^3/$_4$ oz yoghurt butter • 50 g/1^3/$_4$ oz sugar • 1 tsp
grated peel of 1 organic lemon • 3 egg yolks • 50 g/1^3/$_4$ oz
cornflour • 1 tsp baking powder • 500 g/1 lb 2 oz low-fat
curd cheese • 3 egg whites

Place the mandarin oranges in a sieve and leave to drain well.
Slice open the vanilla pod and scrape out the seeds. Add to the
milk and bring to the boil, add the rice, cover with a lid and cook
over a low heat for about 20 minutes. Allow to cool.
Whisk the butter with the sugar and lemon peel until foamy.
Gradually add the egg yolk a little at a time. Add the cornflour
and baking powder to the butter. Stir in the curd cheese and the
cooled rice pudding. Beat the egg whites until stiff and fold in
together with the mandarin oranges. Pour the mixture into a
greased spring-form cake tin (26 cm/10^1/$_2$ in diameter) and
bake in the oven for about 1 hour 15 minutes at 180°C/355ºF/
Gas 4 (fan oven 160°C/320ºF/Gas 3). Cover with baking paper
if necessary.

Preparation time: approx. 45 min., per piece: approx. 9 g P, 5 g F, 19 g C, 166 kcal

TIP

The rice makes this cake especially light and fluffy.
The mandarin oranges can be replaced with berries or cherries.
You can, of course, also use fresh fruit if you wish.

Grape and Lime Compote

Cut **750 g/1 lb 10 oz white grapes** in half, remove the seeds. Top up the **juice of 3 limes** with water to 200 ml/7 fl oz. Bring the grapes and lime juice together with **2 tsp cinnamon** to the boil and simmer over a low heat for about 2 minutes. Add **6 tbsp fruit syrup** and fold in **2 tbsp chopped cashew nuts**. Leave to cool, then serve.

Preparation time: approx. 20 min., per portion: approx. 2 g P, 5 g F, 41 g C, 255 kcal

Chilled Rose Hip Soup

Crush **250 g/9 oz dried rose hips** with a pestle and mortar and soak in water for about 4 hours. Then simmer for about 30 minutes in the soaking water.

Pass the soup through a sieve and top up the liquid with **grape juice** to 1.5 l/ 2½ pints. Stir in **50 g/1 3/4 oz sugar**, bring to the boil and bind with **1 tbsp cornflour** mixed with a little water. Allow the soup to cool down. Season with **1 tbsp honey** and **the juice of ½ lemon**. Pour into bowls and top each with **1 tbsp whipped cream**.

Preparation time: approx. 20 min., per portion: approx. 5 g P, 1 g F, 50 g C, 260 kcal

Pomelo Bake

1–2 pomelo (about 250 g/9 oz) • 2 pears (about 250 g/9 oz)
• 1 tsp butter • 50 ml/1¾ fl oz unsweetened apple juice •
300 ml/11 fl oz low-fat milk • 60 g/2 oz semolina •
1 tbsp amaretto • 1 egg • 6 tbsp muesli without sugar •
3 tbsp honey

Peel the pomelo and pears, fillet the pomelo, remove the cores
from the pears.
Cut the pomelo and pears into small pieces and place in an
ovenproof dish greased with butter. Drizzle with the apple juice
and bake in the oven for about 15 minutes at 200°C/390°F/
Gas 6 (fan oven 180°C/355°F/Gas 4). Bring the milk to the boil,
sprinkle in the semolina and bring back to the boil while stirring.
Remove the pan from the heat, fold in the amaretto and egg
and pour the mixture over the baked fruit. Roast the muesli in
a pan without fat and sprinkle over the bake. Drizzle with the
honey. Bake the dish in the oven for another 35 minutes.

Preparation time: approx. 25 min., per portion: approx. 7 g P, 3 g F, 40 g C, 224 kcal

TIP
The pomelo is a large grapefruit-like citrus fruit with
a thick yellowy-white peel and a sweet acidic taste.
It goes well with the flavour of the pears.

Hot Fruit Salad with Blood Orange

Mix together **3 peeled and filleted oranges** and **2 peeled, cored and diced apples**. While stirring, caramelise **4 tsp vanilla sugar** and **4 tbsp sugar** in **75 g/2½ oz melted butter**. Mix with **the juice of 1 blood orange**. Add the mixed fruit and heat up. Fold **200 g/7 oz frozen raspberries** into the hot fruit salad and heat through. Drizzle with **20 ml/4 tsp raspberry schnapps** and serve sprinkled with **2 tbsp roasted pine kernels**.

Preparation time: approx. 30 min., per portion: approx. 3 g P, 18 g F, 27 g C, 285 kcal

Baked Mango with Cinnamon

Peel **2 ripe mangos**, cut in half, remove the stones and cut the fruit into wedges. Place in a greased ovenproof dish and sprinkle with **60 g/2 oz brown sugar**. Pour in **180 ml/6 fl oz peach juice** and **50 ml/1³⁄₄ fl oz Vin Santo**. Sprinkle with **1 tbsp cinnamon**. Cover the dish with aluminium foil and bake in the oven for about 30 minutes at 180°C/355°F/Gas 4 (fan oven 160°C/320°F/Gas 3).
Reduce the temperature to 150°C/300°F/Gas 2 (fan oven 130°C/265°F/Gas 1/2) and bake for another 20 minutes. If desired, serve with **100 g/3¹⁄₂ oz fat-reduced crème fraîche**.

**Preparation time: approx. 20 min.,
per portion: approx. 1 g P, 7 g F, 28 g C, 191 kcal**

Chunky Oat and Coconut Biscuits

For about 40 biscuits
Whisk **2 egg yolks** until creamy, mix in **2 tbsp sunflower oil** and **150 g/ 5 oz honey**, then add **100 g/3½ oz oat flakes**, **50 g/1¾ oz sesame seeds** and **50 g/1¾ oz each of finely chopped dried pineapple** and **coconut flakes** and work the mixture to a firm consistency. Place about 40 little heaps of this mixture on a greased baking tray. Bake in the oven for about 12 minutes at 180°C/355°F/Gas 4 (fan oven 160°C/320°F/Gas 3).

Preparation time: approx. 20 min., per biscuit: approx. 1 g P, 2 g F, 5 g C, 44 kcal

Crustless Cheesecake

For 10 slices

Mix together **250 g/9 oz low-fat curd cheese, 100g/3½ oz full-cream yoghurt, 9 tbsp fructose, the juice of ½ lemon, 3 tbsp Biobin thickening agent** (carob bean flour) and **1 egg yolk**. Fold in **2 stiffly whipped egg whites**. Pour the mixture into a greased spring-form cake tin (18 cm/7 in diameter), smooth over the top and sprinkle with **30 g/1 oz chopped almonds**. Bake in the oven for about 30 minutes at 200°C/390°F/Gas 6 (fan oven 180°C/355°F/Gas 4). Reduce the heat to 180°C/355°F/Gas 4 and bake for another 20 minutes. Leave to cool in the cake tin.

Preparation time: approx. 20 min., per slice: approx. 5 g P, 2 g F, 1 g C, 53 kcal

Flambéed Strawberries with Green Peppercorns

Heat **250 g/9 oz trimmed and rinsed strawberries** in a pan with **1 tbsp sugar** and **3 tbsp water**, then blend to a purée. Put the strawberry sauce to one side.

In a heated pan, toss **600 g/1 lb 5 oz prepared strawberries** in **3 tbsp sugar** and **the juice of 1 orange**. Add **1 tbsp drained green peppercorns** and stir together. Pour in **50 ml/1¾ fl oz brandy** and ignite. Arrange the strawberries and peppercorns in 4 dessert bowls. Top each bowl with **1 tbsp crème fraîche** and coat with the strawberry sauce.

Preparation time: approx. 20 min., per portion: approx. 2 g P, 2 g F, 23 g C, 161 kcal

Raspberries in Buttermilk Jelly

Soak **4 sheets of white gelatine** in water to soften. Flavour **600 ml/1 pint buttermilk** with **2 tbsp raspberry juice** and **2 tbsp sugar**. Dissolve the squeezed-out gelatine in a little hot water, stir into the buttermilk. Arrange **200 g/7 oz prepared raspberries** in 4 glasses. Top up the glasses with the buttermilk mixture and place in the fridge to set. Serve the buttermilk jelly decorated with **raspberries**.

Preparation time: approx. 20 min., per portion: approx. 6 g P, 1 g F, 11 g C, 87 kcal

Frozen Melon Gateau

For 12 slices

Whisk together **2 eggs, 50 g/1¾ oz sugar** and **2 tsp vanilla sugar** until foamy. Sieve in **50 g/1¾ oz flour** and stir in **30 g/1 oz melted butter**. Pour into a greased spring-form cake (22 cm/9 in diameter) and bake in the oven for about 15 minutes at 180°C/355°F/Gas 4 (fan oven 160°C/320°F/Gas 3). Turn out onto a cake rack and leave to cool. Peel **400 g/14 oz each of both Galia** and **honeydew melons**, remove the seeds and purée the fruit with **the juice of 1 lime**. Mix together **200 ml/7 fl oz low-fat milk, 100 ml/3½ fl oz stiffly whipped cream, 2 tsp gelatine powder, the melon purée** and **1 tsp finely chopped mint leaves**. Spread the cream mixture over the gateau base (surrounded by a cake ring) and freeze in freezer for at least 6 hours. Allow to thaw slightly before serving and garnish with **melon balls**. Mix **1 small packet (2 tsp) of clear gelatine glaze** with **1 tbsp sugar** and **125 ml/4 fl oz melon juice** and spread over the gateau. Allow to set.

Preparation time: approx. 30 min., per piece: approx. 3 g P, 6 g F, 15 g C, 135 kcal

Cream Cheese Cake

For about 12 slices

Mix together **100 g/3½ oz soft butter** and **200 g/7 oz crumbled whole-meal zwieback** and place in a spring-form cake tin (24 cm/10 in diameter) lined with baking paper. Prepare **1 pack jelly** of your choice according to the instructions on the packet with **80 g/3 oz sugar** and **200 ml/7 fl oz water**. Mix together **400 g/14 oz low-fat cream cheese, 250g/9 oz sour cream** and **2 tsp vanilla sugar** and stir in 2/3 of the jelly. Spread **2 peeled and sliced kiwis** over the cake base and cover with the cream cheese mixture. Layer **1 sliced banana** on top of the cream mixture and glaze with the remaining jelly. Chill for 1 hour.

Preparation time: approx. 30 min., per slice: approx. 6 g P, 8 g F, 23 g C, 192 kcal

Curd Cheese and Raspberry Pastries

For 20 pastries
500 g/1 lb 2 oz low-fat curd cheese • 150 ml/5 fl oz low-fat milk • 130 g/4^1/$_2$ oz sugar • 2 tsp vanilla sugar • 1 packet vanilla blancmange powder • 3 tbsp lemon juice • 250 g/9 oz apples • 350 g/12 oz raspberries • 400 g/14 oz flour • 3 tsp baking powder • 100 ml/3^1/$_2$ fl oz vegetable oil • 1 egg • 1 tbsp milk • 100 g/3^1/$_2$ oz icing sugar • flour for the worktop

Mix together 300 g/11 oz curd cheese, 50 ml/1^3/$_4$ fl oz milk, 50 g/1^3/$_4$ oz sugar, the vanilla sugar, the blancmange powder and 1 tbsp lemon juice. Peel the apples, remove the cores and finely dice. Fold the diced apple and prepared raspberries into the curd cheese mixture.

To make the pastry, mix together the flour and baking powder and sieve into a bowl. Add the remaining curd cheese, the remaining milk, the remaining sugar and the oil and mix to a smooth dough using a hand mixer. Roll out the dough on a floured worktop to a thickness of about 3 mm/^{1}/$_{10}$ in and cut out 20 pastry circles (12 cm/5 in diameter). Spoon the curd cheese and fruit mixture onto one half of each circle of pastry. Separate the yolk from the white of the egg, and brush the edges of the pastry with the egg white. Fold the other half of the pastry circle over the filling. Beat the egg yolk with the milk and use to brush the pastries. Place them on a baking tray and bake in the oven for about 20 minutes at 180°C/355ºF/Gas 4 (fan oven 160°C/320ºF/Gas 3).

Mix the icing sugar with the remaining lemon juice and brush over the pastries while still warm. Leave to cool.

Preparation time: approx. 30 min.,

per pastry: approx. 6 g P,

2 g F, 25 g C, 146 kcal

TIP
These delicious pastries can also be filled with other fruit. Why not try out a filling of nuts and oat flakes?

Soured Milk Cake with Fruit

For about 20 slices

Whisk together **150 g/5 oz margarine for baking, 175 g/6 oz sugar** and **2 eggs** until foamy. Stir in **400 g/14 oz soured milk**. Mix **400 g/14 oz flour** with **1 pinch cinnamon, 3 tbsp cocoa powder** and **2 tsp bicarbonate of soda** and stir into the egg mixture. Finally, fold **700 g/1 lb 8 oz drained tinned fruit cocktail** into the mixture. Pour the cake mix into a greased springform cake tin and bake in the oven for about 50 minutes at 170°C/340°F/Gas 3 (fan oven 150°C/300°F/Gas 2). Leave to cool on a cake rack. Dust with **icing sugar** and decorate with **slices of apricot** and **peach**.

Preparation time: approx. 20 min., per slice: approx. 3 g P, 7 g F, 22 g C, 174 kcal

Berry Tart

For about 12 slices

Whisk **2 egg whites** with **1 pinch salt** until stiff, stir in **3 tbsp honey**, fold in **2 egg yolks**. Mix **150 g/5 oz ground almonds** with **2 tbsp cornflour** and mix into the egg mixture. Pour the mixture into a spring-form cake tin (18 cm/7 in diameter) and bake in the oven for about 20 minutes at 180°C/355°F/Gas 4 (fan oven 160°C/320°F/Gas 3). Allow to cool, turn out of the tin and surround with a cake ring. Cover the base with **400 g/14 oz prepared fresh berries** (strawberries, blackberries, raspberries), soak **1 sheet gelatine** to soften, heat in **100 ml/3½ fl oz unsweetened apple juice,** and pour over the berries. Allow to cool, remove the cake ring.

Preparation time: approx. 30 min., per slice: approx. 4 g P, 8 g F, 5 g C, 110 kcal

Yoghurt Tart with Kiwi Fruit and Mango

For 12 slices

Whisk **2 egg whites** together with **2 tbsp water** and **80 g/3 oz sugar** until stiff. Stir **2 egg yolks** together with **50 g/1¾ oz flour, 30 g/1 oz cornflour** and **½ tsp baking powder** into the egg white. Fill the mixture into a spring-form cake tin (24 cm/9 1/2 in diameter) lined with baking paper and bake in the oven for about 25 minutes at 200°C/390°F/Gas 6 (fan oven 180°C/355°F/Gas 4). Turn out onto a cake rack and pull away the paper. When cooled, cut in half horizontally, save one half for some other use. Soak **10 sheets white gelatine** to soften, then dissolve in **20 ml/4 tsp heated orange liqueur** and stir into **250 g/9 oz low-fat yoghurt**. Allow to set in a bowl with iced water. Stir in 1 egg white stiffly whisked with **20 g/¾ oz sugar**, and **125 ml/4 fl oz stiffly whipped cream**. Fold **1 peeled and diced mango** and **4 peeled and diced kiwi fruit** into the mixture. Brush the cake base with **2 tbsp orange marmelade**, smoothly spread the yoghurt and fruit cream on top. Decorate with **pieces of fruit**.

Preparation time: approx. 25 min., per slice: approx. 3 g P, 5 g F, 16 g C, 132 kcal

Fruity Soufflés

For 12 soufflés

Stir **200 g/7 oz drained low-fat curd cheese** together with **5 egg yolks** until creamy, mix with **1 tsp salt** and **4 tbsp cornflour**. Whisk **5 egg whites** until very stiff and fold into the egg yolk mixture. Grease 12 ramekins (10 cm/4 in diameter) and spoon 1 tbsp of the mixture into each. Prepare **250 g/9 oz fruit** (for example rhubarb, cherries, grapes) and place 1 tbsp of fruit in the middle of each ramekin. Cover with the curd cheese and egg mixture and bake in the oven for about 45 minutes at 175°C/350°F/Gas 4 (fan oven 150°C/300°F/Gas 2). Do not open the oven door during baking. Serve warm.

Preparation time: approx. 20 min., per soufflé: approx. 5 g P, 3 g F, 2 g C, 60 kcal

Jellied Apricots and Redcurrants

Bring to the boil **250 ml/9 fl oz apricot nectar** with **1 tsp sugar** and **the seeds (scrapes) from 1 vanilla pod**. Mix **3 tbsp cornflour** in **a little water** and while stirring use to bind the nectar. Add 2 tsp grated organic lemon peel and **1 tbsp lemon juice** and leave to cool.

Skin **250 g/9 oz fresh apricots**, cut in half, remove the stones and cut the fruit into pieces. Heat up in the apricot nectar together with **100 g/3½ oz each of redcurrants** and **blackberries**, and use to fill rinsed individual jelly moulds. Place in the fridge to set. Turn out onto plates and serve each portion with spoonful of **yoghurt**.

Preparation time: approx. 30 min., per portion: approx. 1 g P, 1 g F, 9 g C, 39 kcal

Baked Bananas with Coconut Yoghurt

Warm **75 ml/2½ fl oz orange juice** with **1 tbsp sugar** and mix with **1 tsp cornflour** dissolved in **a little water**. While stirring, add **250 g/9 oz drained tinned pineapple chunks** and simmer for 2 minutes until the juice thickens. Pour the pineapple sauce over **2 peeled and halved bananas** in an oven-proof dish and bake in the oven for about 10 minutes at 200°C/390°F/Gas 6. Mix **150 g/5 oz yoghurt** with **1 tbsp coconut milk, 1 tsp lemon juice, 1 egg white** and **100 ml/3½ fl oz cream**, both whipped until stiff, and serve with the bananas.

Preparation time: approx. 35 min., per portion: approx. 4 g P, 9 g F, 36 g C, 248 kcal

Wholemeal Cake with Apple and Blackberry and Crunchy Brittle

For about 10 slices
350 g/12 oz apples • 3 tbsp lemon juice • 300 g/11 oz
wholemeal wheat flour • 3$\frac{1}{2}$ tsp cream of tartar • 1 tsp
ground cinnamon • 150 g/5 oz sugar • 1 egg • 200 g/
7 oz low-fat cream cheese • 175 g/6 oz blackberries •
60 g/2 oz brown sugar cubes • fat to grease the tin

Peel the apples, remove the cores, and dice the fruit. Sprinkle
immediately with the lemon juice and bring to the boil in a
saucepan. Simmer for 10 minutes while stirring, then allow to
cool.
Sieve the flour with the cream of tartar and cinnamon into a
bowl, stir in the sugar. Fold in the egg, the cream cheese and
the cooled cooked apples. Work everything to a smooth mixture.
Fold in 115 g/4 oz prepared blackberries. Crush the sugar cubes
with a rolling pin and sprinkle into a greased loaf tin. Spread the
remaining blackberries on top of the sugar, add the cake mixture
and smooth over the top. Bake the cake in the oven for about
45 minutes at 190°C/375°F/Gas 5 (fan oven 170°C/3400F/
Gas 3). Allow to cool, then turn out of the loaf tin.

Preparation time: approx. 40 min., per slice: approx. 6 g P, 8 g F, 44 g C, 280 kcal

TIP

Try out this delicious wholemeal cake with other
berries, for example raspberries, blueberries
or blackcurrants. Replace the cooked apples with
cooked pears or quinces.

Colourful Fruit Kebabs

Peel **2 bananas** and **2 kiwi fruit** and cut into slices. Remove the cores from **2 pears** and **2 nectarines** and cut into wedges. Together with **12 black grapes** and **8 drained tinned mandarin orange segments**, thread the pieces of fruit onto wooden skewers and arrange on plates.
Caramelise in a pan **6 tbsp orange juice** and **the grated peel of 1 organic orange** with **4 tbsp sugar** and drizzle over the fruit skewers while still runny. Drizzle with **Cointreau**, flambé and serve immediately.

Preparation time: approx. 15 min., per portion: approx. 2 g P, 1 g F, 47 g C, 215 kcal

Curd Cheese with Apricots

Skin **8 apricots**, remove the stones and cut the fruit into wedges. Cut **¼ bunch peppermint leaves** into thin strips, mix with the apricot wedges and drizzle everything with **20 ml/4 tsp apricot liqueur**. Stir together **200g/7 oz low-fat curd cheese** and **a little milk** and sweeten with **1 tsp sugar**. Stiffly whip **100 ml/3½ fl oz cream** and fold into the curd cheese. Divide up the curd cheese between 4 dessert dishes and spread the apricots and their liquid on top.

Preparation time: approx. 20 min., per portion: approx. 8 g P, 8 g F, 14 g C, 170 kcal

Pear Helene

Peel **4 small pears**, remove the cores and gently simmer the fruit in **150 ml/ 5 fl oz water** until soft. Mix **2 tbsp chocolate blancmange powder** with **60 ml/4 tbsp low-fat milk**, bring to the boil and add **1–2 tbsp sugar** according to taste. Arrange the pear halves on 4 plates and coat with the chocolate sauce.

Preparation time: approx. 20 min., per portion: approx. 3 g P, 4 g F, 25 g C, 152 kcal

Apple Pasties

For 16 pasties

Mix to a smooth dough **125 g/4¹/2 oz flour, 1 egg yolk, 125 g/4¹/2 oz drained curd cheese, 1 pinch salt** and **125 g/4 1/2 oz low-fat margarine**, wrap in cling film and put in the fridge to stand for 30 minutes. Grate **500 g/1 lb 2 oz peeled and cored apples**, mix together with **2 tbsp sugar, 2 tbsp Calvados** and **1 tbsp lemon juice**. Fold in **30 g/1 oz chopped walnuts** and **30 g/1 oz raisins**. Roll out the pastry to a rectangle, fold over both outer thirds to the middle and roll out once again. Repeat this procedure twice, then roll the pasty out until quite thin and cut out 16 circles of pastry (12 cm/5 in diameter). Place 1 tbsp apple filling in the middle of each circle, brush the edges with **egg white** and fold over to form pasties. Bake in the oven for about 20 minutes at 200°C/390ºF/Gas 6 (fan oven 180°C/355ºF/ Gas 4).

Preparation time: approx. 55 min., per piece: approx. 2 g P, 8 g F, 11 g C, 132 kcal

Crêpes with Flambéed Strawberries

Prepare a batter with **50 g/1¾ oz flour, 1 tbsp sugar, 1 pinch salt, grated organic lemon peel** and **125 ml/4 fl oz low-fat milk** and allow to stand for 20 minutes. Fold in **1 egg** and **1 egg yolk.** In a greased frying pan, fry 4–6 thin crêpes. Keep warm.

Cut in half **500 g/1 lb 2 oz prepared strawberries**, drizzle with **2 tbsp runny honey** and flambé with **4 tbsp rum**. Fold **2 tbsp quince jelly** into the strawberries. Spread the fruit over the crêpes, fold in half and serve sprinkled with **roasted pistachios**.

Preparation time: approx. 30 min., per portion: approx. 6 g P, 5 g F, 27 g C, 131 kcal

Fruit Gratin

Divide **450 g/1 lb fresh fruit** of the season, for example strawberries, cherries, peaches, blackcurrants, into 4 individual gratin dishes. Mix **150 g/ 5 oz each of low-fat double cream** and **low-fat cream cheese** with **5 drops vanilla flavouring** and pour over the fruit. Sprinkle **1 tbsp sugar** over each dish. Bake under a hot oven grill until the sugar caramelises. Serve hot.

Preparation time: approx. 25 min., per portion: approx. 6 g P, 12 g F, 9 g C, 179 kcal

Red Fruit Jelly with Vanilla Yoghurt

Remove and set aside **6 tbsp juice** from a **380 g/13½ oz jar or tin of morello cherries**. Place the remaining juice and cherries in a saucepan together with **250 g/9 oz halved strawberries** and **250 g/9 oz cleaned and sorted redcurrants**. Add **3 tbsp sugar**, **½ tsp cinnamon** and **½ vanilla pod** and bring to the boil.

Mix the retained cherry juice with **1 packet vanilla blancmange powder** and add to the boiling fruit, then bring to the boil once again. Divide the fruit jelly into 4 portions in little dishes, and when cold serve each dish decorated with **3 tbsp vanilla yoghurt** (in total about 300 g/11 oz).

Preparation time: approx. 25 min., per portion: approx. 2 g P, 10 g F, 15 g C, 169 kcal

Vanilla Cream with Blueberries

Soften **8 sheets white gelatine** in cold water for about 10 minutes.
Mix in a saucepan **300 ml/11 fl oz low-fat milk, 2 tsp vanilla, 1 tbsp grated lime peel** and **2 tbsp sugar** and heat for about 2 minutes. Remove from the heat, add the squeezed gelatine to the hot liquid and dissolve while stirring. Allow to cool down, then stir in **100 ml/3½ fl oz soured milk.** From **400 g/14 oz blueberries** put a few berries to one side, purée the rest and fold into the vanilla cream. Put the cream in the fridge to set and serve decorated with the remaining blueberries.

Preparation time: approx. 15 min., per portion: approx. 13 g P, 1 g F, 19 g C, 154 kcal

Wholemeal Crêpes with Fruit Purée

125 g/4 1/2 oz wholemeal wheat flour · 2 tbsp honey ·
1 pinch salt · 1 tbsp walnut oil · 1 tbsp coconut flakes ·
3 eggs · 125 ml/4 1/2 fl oz milk · 300 g/11 oz pineapple ·
1 tbsp white rum · 1 tbsp yoghurt · 1 tbsp honey · 2 tbsp
butter

Prepare a smooth batter with the sieved wholemeal flour, honey, salt, walnut oil, coconut flakes, eggs and 125 ml/4½ fl oz each of water and milk and leave to stand for 30 minutes.

Peel the pineapple, remove the hard core and eyes, and purée the fruit in a liquidiser together with the rum. Mix the fruit purée with the yoghurt and honey.

In a frying pan, fry 6–8 thin crêpes from the batter in 2 tbsp butter, drain on kitchen paper and stack on a plate. Cut 1 crêpe into strips.

Place 1–2 tbsp fruit purée in the middle of a crêpe, gather up the edges and tie together at the top with a strip of crêpe to form a pouch. Repeat the process for the remaining crêpes.

Preparation time: approx. 40 min., per portion: approx. 5 g P, 7 g F, 20 g C, 176 kcal

TIP

These crêpe pouches taste delicious with chocolate sauce. To make it, melt 30 g/1 oz grated dark chocolate and stir into 250 ml/9 fl oz heated low-fat milk.

Filled Melon

Cut in half **2 honeydew melons** and remove the seeds. Scoop out the flesh up to about 1 cm/$^1/_3$ in from the skin and dice the fruit. Place the melon halves in the fridge to keep cool.

Cut in half **200 g/7 oz each of both strawberries** and **cherries**, remove the stones from the cherries. Peel and dice **1–2 kiwi fruit**. Also dice **200 g/ 7 oz pineapple**. Mix all the fruit together with **5 tbsp orange juice** and **125 g/4$^1/_2$ oz sugar** and chill for about 30 minutes. Use to fill the melon halves and serve.

Preparation time: approx. 20 min.,

per portion: approx. 2 g P, 1 g F, 33 g C, 328 kcal

Mango with Strawberry Sauce

Peel **2 large ripe mangoes**, separate the fruit from the stones and cut the fruit into thin wedges. Arrange fan-like on 4 dishes and drizzle with **the juice of ¹/₂ lime.** Blend together to a purée **400 g/14 oz strawberries, 2 tbsp lime juice, 4 tbsp icing sugar** and **20 ml/4 tbsp orange liqueur**. Pass the sauce through a sieve and mix together with **4 tbsp cream yoghurt.** Pour over the mango wedges.

Preparation time: approx. 20 min., per portion: approx. 2 g P, 2 g F, 21 g C, 132 kcal

Strawberry Roulade

For 12 slices

Prepare a cake mixture by mixing together **3 egg yolks, 115 g/4 oz sugar, 115 g/4 oz flour** and **3 tbsp water** and folding in **3 stiffly whisked egg whites.** Spread over a greased baking tray and bake in the oven for about 10 minutes at 220°C/430°F/Gas 7 (fan oven 200°C/390°F/Gas 6). Turn out onto a sugared kitchen cloth, roll up together and allow to cool. Purée **200 g/7 oz low-fat cream cheese** with **250 g/9 oz strawberries** and **1 tbsp sugar**. Unroll the cake, spread with the cream cheese and strawberry mixture. Top with **150 g/5 oz strawberries** cut into small pieces. With the help of the cloth, roll up the cake and place in the fridge to chill.

Preparation time: approx. 40 min., per portion: approx. 5 g P, 2 g F, 18 g C, 119 kcal

Fresh Fruit Soup

Remove the stones from **300 g/11 oz washed cherries**, cut **200 g/ 7 oz trimmed and sorted strawberries** in half. Mix both fruits together along with **200 g/7 oz raspberries, 200 g/7 oz blackcurrants** and **200 g/ 7 oz blackberries** and arrange in dessert bowls. Bring to the boil **250 ml/ 9 fl oz red grape juice**, mix **1 tbsp cornflour** with **a little water** and use to bind the grape juice. Bring to the boil, sweeten with either **2 tsp vanilla sugar** or **honey** and pour over the fruit. Set in the fridge to chill.

Preparation time: approx. 30 min., per portion: approx. 3 g P, 1 g F, 31 g C, 171 kcal

Chilled Yoghurt Soup with Berries

Mix together in a bowl **250 g/9 oz fruit flavoured yoghurt drink** (for example blackberry/bilberry) and **a few mint leaves** cut into strips. Chill for 30 minutes.

Chill **400 g/14 oz prepared fresh bilberries** and **blackberries** in the freezer until they are almost frozen. Fold into the yoghurt drink and serve in dessert bowls garnished with **a few mint leaves**.

Preparation time: approx. 15 min., per portion: approx. 3 g P, 3 g F, 5 g C, 73 kcal

Berry Sorbet

Purée in a liquidiser **400 g/14 oz frozen mixed berries** with **4 tbsp sugar**, **2 tbsp lime juice** and **2 tbsp orange liqueur** until a creamy mixture is achieved. Portion the sorbet into 4 small dishes and serve immediately. Garnish with **fresh berries**.

Preparation time: approx. 10 min., per portion: approx. 1 g P, 1 g F, 13 g C, 76 kcal

Summer Jelly

Place in a bowl **500 g/1 lb 2 oz prepared blackberries**
and **6 nectarines** cut into thin wedges and coat with a mixture of **30 g/1 oz
acacia honey, 2 tbsp lime juice**, and **2 tbsp unsweetened red grape juice**.
Leave to stand for 30 minutes.
Stir together **750 ml/1¹/₃ pints pear juice** and **60 g/2 oz pearl sago**
and simmer over a low heat until the sago becomes transparent. Remove
from the heat and allow to cool. Fold the marinated fruit into the pear sago
and spoon into glass bowls. Serve each bowl topped with **1 tbsp thickly
whipped cream**.

Preparation time: approx. 20 min., per portion: approx. 3 g P, 2 g F, 44 g C, 214 kcal

Muesli Gateau with Pear Cream

For 16 slices

Roast **200 g/7 oz muesli base mixture without sugar** in a pan without fat.
Mix together with **100 g/3 1/2 oz melted butter** and **50 g/1¾ oz honey**.
Spread the muesli mixture over a cake plate the size of a spring-form cake
tin (26 cm/10½ in diameter).
Place the spring-form cake tin without its base around the cake plate. Drain
375 g/13 oz tinned pears. Soften **10 sheets white gelatine** in water,
squeeze to remove excess water and dissolve in **6 tbsp heated pear juice**.
Mix together **250 g/9 oz low-fat curd cheese, 500 g/1 lb 2 oz soured
milk, 100 g/3½ oz sugar** and **2 tbsp orange juice**, fold in the finely diced
pears. Mix the gelatine with 3 tbsp of the mixture, then stir in the remaining
pear cream. Whip **200 ml/7 fl oz cream** until stiff and fold into the mixture.
Spread the fruit cream over the muesli base and chill for 3 hours. Release the
spring form. Sprinkle with **chocolate vermicelli**.

Preparation time: approx. 40 min., per slice: approx. 5 g P, 7 g F, 22 g C, 180 kcal

Raspberry Pavlova

For 4 pavlovas
2 egg whites • 1 tsp cornflour • 1 tsp raspberry vinegar •
100 g/3½ oz sugar • 2 tbsp cranberry jelly • 2 tbsp unsweetened orange juice • 1 tsp grated peel of 1 organic orange •
150 g/5 oz low-fat cream cheese or ricotta • 175 g/6 oz
raspberries

Whisk the egg whites until stiff, mix with the cornflour and
vinegar.
Add the sugar a little at a time and stir to a firm and shiny
mixture. Separate the egg white mixture into 4 portions. Leaving
enough space between them, spread each portion as a 10 cm/
4 in diameter circle on a baking tray lined with baking paper.
Bake in the oven for about 45 minutes at 150°C/300°F/Gas 2
(fan oven 130°C/265°F/Gas 1/2) until the mixture has become
crisp and lightly browned.
In the meantime, heat the cranberry jelly in a saucepan together
with the orange juice and peel, and stir until dissolved.
Leave to cool. Remove the meringues from the baking tray and
arrange on plates. Spread with the cream cheese and layer with
the prepared raspberries. Top with the cranberry jelly sauce and
serve immediately.

Preparation time: approx. 20 min., per pavlova: approx. 7 g P, 1 g F, 33 g C, 178 kcal

TIP

Instead of baking 4 small meringues, you can also fill little ovenproof moulds with the egg white and top with cream cheese and
fruit when baked. You can also replace the cream cheese with low-
fat curd cheese and enhance it with orange juice or raspberry juice.

Papaya Salad with Exotic Spices

Peel **2 ripe papayas**, cut in half and scoop out the seeds. First cut the fruit in slices then strips, place in a saucepan together with **150 g/5 oz sugar, the seeds (scraped) from 1 vanilla pod, 125 ml/4 fl oz water, 2 tbsp ginger syrup, 1 generous pinch ground cloves, 1 pinch cinnamon** and **1 pinch chilli powder,** bring to the boil, simmer for 10 minutes and then leave to cool. Peel **1 grapefruit,** fillet the segments, mix together with the papaya and its cooking liquid and **the juice of 1 lemon.** Arrange in dishes. Drizzle with **20 ml/4 tsp coconut syrup** and serve garnished with **1 tbsp thinly grated slices of coconut.**

Preparation time: approx. 30 min., per portion: approx. 1 g P, 2 g F, 48 g C, 222 kcal

Baked Papaya

Peel **2 large papayas**, cut in half, scoop out the seeds and cut the fruit into wedges. Mix together **4 egg yolks, 100g/3½ oz each of curd cheese and double cream, 2 tsp vanilla sugar, 1 tbsp ground ginger** and **2 tbsp brown sugar.**

Lay the papaya wedges in a greased ovenproof dish, spread the egg mixture on top and bake in the oven for about 20 minutes at 220°C/430°F/Gas 7 (fan oven 200°C/390°F/Gas 6).

Sprinkle with **2 tbsp chopped pistachios** before serving.

Preparation time: approx. 20 min., per portion: approx. 8 g P, 17 g F, 9 g C, 229 kcal

Fruit and Semolina Slices

For about 12 slices

Bring to the boil **750 ml/1¹/₃ pints milk** with **1 pinch salt, 3 tbsp honey** and **the grated peel of 1 organic lemon**, stir in **150 g/5 oz semolina**, simmer for 5 minutes and then allow to stand until the semolina has swollen. Stir **2 egg yolks** into the semolina and fold in **2 stiffly whisked egg whites**. Also fold in **4 peeled, cored and diced pears** together with **¹/₂ tsp cardamom**. Spread the mixture onto a baking tray lined with baking paper, sprinkle with **3 tbsp sesame seeds** and bake in the oven for about 20 minutes at 220°C/430°F/Gas 7 (fan oven 200°C/390°F/Gas 6). Cut into 12 slices and serve with **fruit sauce**.

Preparation time: approx. 40 min., per slice: approx. 3 g P, 4 g F, 11 g C, 100 kcal

Strawberry and Sesame Dumplings on Apricot Cream

For 12 dumplings

Mix together **200 g/7 oz low-fat curd cheese, 50 g/1³/₄ oz low-fat margarine, 1 egg, 50 g/1³/₄ oz sugar, 1 pinch salt**, and **a little grated lemon peel**. Sieve in **150 g/5 oz flour** and mix together. Roll out the dough until ¹/₂ cm/¹/₆ in thick, cut into 12 squares (each twice the size of a strawberry). Lay **1 prepared strawberry** on each square, wrap the dough around the fruit and simmer in boiling water for about 10 minutes.

Remove, drain, and coat in **30 g/1 oz sesame seeds.** Skin **250 g/9 oz ripe apricots**, remove the stones, purée the fruit together with **20 ml/4 tsp apricot liqueur** and **2 tbsp sugar,** and serve with the strawberry dumplings.

Preparation time: approx. 40 min., per dumpling: approx. 4 g P, 5 g F, 17 g C, 137 kcal